Lead from the Front

101 Leadership Quips, Quotes and Anecdotes That Will Impact
Your Career and Your Life

Jim Lipuma

ISBN : 1495910660
ISBN 13: 9781495910661

Dedicated to my amazing family:

Diane, my soulmate, who provides unconditional love and support, and who convinced me that the time is now to write my first book

Alyssa and Carly, who provide motivation and inspiration every day

Leading a team of people, especially salespeople, can be frustrating, challenging, and disheartening. It also can be rewarding, exhilarating, and fulfilling. Done right, you can gain the allegiance, trust, and confidence of your people, achieve tremendous results, and find your way to the top of your organization.

In *Lead from the Front*, you will be exposed to 101 powerful tips that will help you sidestep challenges, take advantage of opportunities, and put yourself in a position to achieve at a high level and move up the corporate ladder. You will find that these anecdotes will apply to your personal and professional life and will help you grow both as a person and as a professional.

Lead from the Front will transform you into a leader who will be able to change the dynamic within your team and allow you to form a bond with team members unlike you have ever experienced before.

Contents

Jim Lipuma

Preface

In preparing to write this book, I reflected on my career. I thought about my first "real" job as an inside sales rep for R. H. Donnelley. I thought about how I progressed through my career and about the people who were most influential in my formative years. I watched my first manager teach with great passion and embrace his people. He shared the same tips with every person, yet some moved forward, while others fell aside. At the time, I focused on my activities and thought my efforts would carry me forward. I felt that if I outworked everyone else, I would rise to the top quickly. Work ethic is certainly an important component of success, but there is so much more. You see, our manager shared the same information, in pretty much the same way, but some people grabbed onto it, while others felt they had a better way. Those who followed the process progressed. Those who charted their own path departed.

After several years of working in inside and outside sales, I was tapped on the shoulder to lead a team. Being young and naïve, and having a few strong years of sales success, I thought, *How hard could this be?* I figured everybody wanted to succeed and all I had to do was show the way and they would be successful. Immediately, I realized that there was this little thing called "personalities," and I would have to manage those personalities—all differently. I also realized that people didn't always want success, or better said, weren't willing to put forth the effort necessary to find success. I found that some people approached their business with an air of entitlement. In short order, I realized that to be successful in a leadership capacity, I was going to have to learn, adapt, and change.

Over the past thirty years, I have been blessed to have been associated with some of the best, most passionate, most committed, and most driven professionals one could hope to work with. I have learned (and continue to learn) from some of the most talented business leaders in corporate America. I have worked in start-ups, Fortune 500 companies, organizations experiencing great growth, and some going through the pain of workforce reduction. Through the years, I have been a student. I have observed how to deal with pressure, implement a process, and drive team unity. Leadership is part art, part skill, and a lot of will. In the coming pages, I share common principles and tidbits of information that will help you become a stronger leader. I believe many of these anecdotes will transfer over to your personal life and help you grow as an individual. They have certainly helped me. Some tips will come naturally, and some will take work. Overall, if you practice and implement what you read in this book, I am confident that you will be rewarded with a tighter team and forward progression in your career. Enjoy.

1

Lead from the Front

—∿—

I n reflecting on the many amazing leaders in the history of our great country, I think about Abraham Lincoln and the courage it took to stand for what was right. I think about Dr. Martin Luther King, Jr., and his willingness to stand in the face of imminent danger to advance his beliefs. I think about Vince Lombardi and his "refuse to lose" attitude. Great leaders put themselves out front and in the direct line of fire. Great leaders stand ground with their people when lesser leaders would flee. Great leaders have a voice and use it, even when they may be standing alone.

One of my favorite movies of all time is *Braveheart*. It is the story of William Wallace, a thirteenth-century Scottish warrior who led the Scots in the first war of Scottish independence against King Edward I of England. Although it was likely embellished a bit for ratings, the core of the story resonates with me. Here we have a man who stands boldly against status quo and historical acceptance. Based on his commitment to his principles, people follow him and fight for him. They are willing to die for him. In the epic battles, William Wallace is dead center and out front at the start of each battle. It is a reminder that people follow those who stand with confidence and conviction and who are willing to stand front and center during the most challenging of situations.

In business, we must understand the mission and truly internalize it. To sell it, we must embrace it or we will come off as inauthentic, and nothing inspires mediocrity more than being less than fully transparent and authentic. You are the leader of your business. Leading from the front takes great courage and the willingness to open yourself up to scrutiny and potential challenge. Without this confidence and courage, your team will not rally behind you. If you put yourself out there, and do it with conviction, your team will follow you through fire. We must be the conduit between those above us and those who report to us. We must all align with the mission of the organization and stay away from words like "they" and, instead, make "we" the cornerstone of our communication. Consistency in our alignment breeds confidence.

Challenge people behind closed doors and fully support them in public. Show no hesitation in supporting your organization's mission and standards. Leading from the front involves much more than simply having a title of "manager." In order to truly be seen as a leader, action, open support and personal accountability must be at the forefront. Lead from the front, and your team will follow.

2

You Work for Your Family

—⁓—

When I first started working for R. H. Donnelley in 1985, I was in new-hire training, completing introductions. One of the questions we were asked was "Who will you be working for?" In a group of twenty-five people, twenty-four answered by stating the name of their direct supervisor. One woman answered by stating, "I work for my customers." I loved this answer, and it has stuck with me all of these years.

I am blessed to have been married to my wife for more than twenty-six years. For more than twenty-three years, we have watched our daughters grow into wonderful women and contributors to society. I realized, through those years, that while working for our clients is critical, necessary, and noble, I clearly discovered that I work for my family. I spring out of bed in the morning knowing that it is for my family that I will drive hard this day. Although my family would never place this burden on me, I realize the role I play and the responsibility I have to them in giving my all every day and achieving at the highest possible level. There is no higher motivation for me. I report to someone, but I am driven by one thing—my family. I will succeed because my family's well-being depends on it.

Put a picture of what matters most in front of you at your desk. Next time you want to cut out early or skip a few calls, think about what matters most and whom you work for. When it is personal, you will find that you have renewed energy and motivation.

3

It's All about the People

—◊—

In today's business environment, there is an intense focus on profit. Without question, profit allows companies to keep and add employees. Profit provides paychecks for employees. Without profit, companies fail and employees find themselves on the outside, looking in.

Although it is not a novel idea, our focus must be on people because employees are the fuel that drives the business and propels profit. I would take this one step further: We must focus intently on the *needs* of our people. Without great people, we will fail. We must find the best talent, invest in their growth and development, and connect with them on multiple levels, both personally and professionally. We have a responsibility to both our employees and our organization to do so.

In our world today, employees have choices and are being presented with new opportunities every day. It is well documented that people leave supervisors at a much higher rate than they leave companies. We must embrace our responsibility to connect with our employees, make them the center of our personal universe, and create a culture in which they flourish and feel valued. If they don't feel connected, they will find that connection somewhere else, and nothing is more painful than watching talent go out the door. I have had great people leave my organization, and I am in physical pain every time. The key is to learn where we fell short and ensure that we improve going forward. You cannot cut corners when it comes to your people.

Go overboard. Your employees are the lifeblood of your organization.

4

Heart Count vs. Head Count

—ɯ—

In a previous role, an organization I worked for was being sold to a private equity firm. We found ourselves in a place where we had to make some difficult decisions regarding personnel. In the early stages of discussions, the idea of heart count vs. head count shone clearly to me. I found myself focused on the people, while the PE firm was firmly rooted in reducing costs and driving profits, in the very near term. Although I saw a path to profitability that could minimize personnel disruption, ultimately the decision was made to displace employees. I realized, at that point, that our strategies were not aligned and were likely never going to intersect. It was time for me to move on.

I tell this story because it is the reality in our world today. Although a focus on cost containment is critical, we cannot lose sight that we are talking about people's lives here and that the term "head count" should be replaced with the term "heart count."

Day in and day out, as you make tough decisions, always keep your people at the center of your thought process. Heart count will keep you focused on the personal nature of your business and the decisions you make.

5

Know Whom You Serve and Serve Them Well

—⚡—

Earlier, I discussed the concept of working for your family. Hand in hand with that principle lies the thought that you work for those you serve. If you are a salesperson, you serve your clients. If you are a manager, you serve your people. If you are a VP, you serve your managers. We must be keenly conscious of whom we serve and serve them with great integrity, true compassion, and committed conviction.

Managing "up" is the antithesis of this concept. All too often, I see people more focused on shining brightly in the eyes of their supervisor than delighting in meeting the needs of their direct reports. If we focus on our people, the rest will take care of itself. Your people are your priority. Remember, they are your customers. If you take care of your customers (your employees), they will take care of their customers (their clients), and in the end, we all win.

6

Their Goal Is Your Goal

—m—

Traditionally, a sales manager's goal is a roll-up of his or her direct reports' individual goals. Success is determined by how well the collective goal is met. In other words, if a manager has a monthly goal of $100,000 in new business and the manager achieves at $110,000, for the month, she has achieved at 110 percent of her monthly goal. Sounds like a great job, right? Not necessarily. You actually have to dig deeper, to gain a true perspective. Follow me on this.

Let's say the manager had ten reps, and each of them had monthly goals of $10,000 each, bringing the team's monthly goal to $100,000. Five of the reps sold $15,000, and the other five sold $7,500. Would you still say the manager did a great job? The manager was 112 percent to goal after all, right? In my world, this is a failing job because half of the sales force achieved only 75 percent of their individual goal. As leaders, we have a responsibility to ensure success for all of our people. Anything less than a 100 percent individual success rate, should be seen as a gap which needs to be closed.

To effect change, you must tie compensation to the result you seek. A common phrase is "pay for performance." Determine what is important, and tailor the compensation goals to influence and align with the company goals. If we truly believe in the principle that we work for those we serve, then in this example, we failed half of our clients. In school, a 50 percent grade is failing, so why shouldn't we mirror that grading system in our workplace? If we want to focus on our people, then we must tie our leadership compensation directly to ensuring achievement of this most critical goal... complete success for all of our people.

7

No Man/Woman Left Behind

—⁓—

C ontinuing with our previous principle, I offer up the idea that as leaders, we have a responsibility to ensure success for each of our people on a monthly, quarterly, and annual basis. To ensure complete and consistent success, as well as reduce employee churn, as leaders we must focus on the idea of leaving nobody behind. This mantra is used in the military; I believe it should be followed in business as well.

I introduced this principle in a previous company and have used it ever since. If a manager has a goal that is tied to the roll-up goal of his people, he will focus on that number only. He will be recognized as an achiever and believe that he is doing a bang-up job, should he over-deliver on his overall team goal. To some degree, he is doing well, but only if we focus on his own goal. The key is to shed light on how each of his people are performing...individually. I propose that we view leadership success in a different way.

Here's a way to change the trajectory of your business, in terms of both focus and revenue. Take 30 percent of a manager's compensation and tie it to the percentage of people on his team who over-deliver on their goal in the given recognition period. If fewer than 70 percent of the manager's people over-deliver on their goal, he misses that part of his bonus. At 70 percent, the manager gets 80 percent of his payout. At 80 percent, the manager gets 90 percent of that portion of his bonus. At 90 percent achievement, the manager gets 120 percent of his bonus on that piece of his bonus, and if 100 percent of his people over-deliver, the manager receives a 150 percent payout on that portion of his plan. This will force the manager to focus on individual rep success versus solely the collective team goal, and it will motivate the leadership team to focus on the success of their individuals. It works. Try it. Before you know it, your team members will feel that they are a priority, managers will connect much more deeply with each of their team members, you will reduce churn, and your company will be flying high.

8

Who Are "They?"

—∿∿—

Have you ever heard an employee say something like, "They decided to change our goals" or "They put this new policy in place." Every time I hear this, I ask one question: "Who are 'they'?"

In the first section, I spoke about leading from the front. A key to being a great leader is to internalize and embrace the company mission and ensure that we individually own every decision. It is our responsibility, as leaders, to share that change in vision or direction, as if we wrote it because if we internalize it, we really did write it. For a team to trust both the organization and the leader, there must be continuity and alignment. When you hear the word "they," just pause and ask the question "Who are 'they'?" Your team members will eventually eliminate this term from their vocabulary. You will effectively do away with the divisive "us" versus "them" mentality. To be one team, we must act and speak as one team. "We" accomplishes this.

9

The Power of "We"

—⁓—

"We the people of the United States of America…."
Doesn't that have such a nice ring to it? There is
power in the word "we." There is a bond in the word "we."
There is a commonality of purpose in the word "we."

Consciously eliminating the word "they" and instead
incorporating the word "we" into daily language will have a
dramatic and long-lasting effect on your team and your business. "We" signifies that we are in this together and that we
are part of the same team.

This principle extends well beyond your individual team.
Think about the other divisions and units that support your
efforts. They are part of "we." Incorporate them into discussions. Bring guests into your team meetings. The more
exposure your people receive to other key contributors and
partners, in other key units, the more that they will understand their place in the greater scheme.

In one company I was with, we used the term "OTOG," which stands for One Team, One Goal. That is a powerful statement and one that resonated with the people. Each of us plays key roles, and every person shoulders weight, much like every player on a football team has a specific responsibility. Bill Belichick, the coach for the New England Patriots, frequently reminds his players to "Do your job." If each person knows his or her role, owns the role, and focuses on perfecting it, the team wins. Sure, Tom Brady plays an important role, but he cannot do his job if his linemen don't block or if his receivers don't run crisp and intelligent routes. Everyone plays a role, and every team member must realize that he or she is just one of many pieces of the puzzle. When we understand our place and focus on our unique role, we will ensure a successful outcome.

10

The Company Is King

—⟋⟍—

We are taught, early in our careers, that we must focus on the WIIFM (what's in it for me) of the people we serve and find a way to align our organization's needs with individuals' needs. In other words, to get buy-in from one of our reps, we must first find a way to show that any change results in a benefit to her. I believe that effective leadership calls for a balance between meeting the needs of the people and meeting the needs of the company, with the company being "king."

This is a bit of a "left turn" compared to what we have been taught and what I have discussed earlier in the book ("It's all about the people"), but an equally important point. Here's the logic: If we make decisions that ultimately do not benefit the organization, we put the livelihoods of every employee at risk. Now, I know this sounds heavy and dramatic, but it is an important point to grasp. Effective leadership entails placing the needs of the organization first. Without a focus on our organization, it may fail to exist. We must understand the impact every decision has on our organization, regardless of how insignificant it seems, and we must be able to ingrain that way of thinking into our culture. Again, this is an area in which consistency is important. When we treat the company as king, we build a business that is centered on all employees versus a few. The next time one of your reps looks for an exception, redirect her to think in terms of how this decision may affect the organization and ask her to share how that move would benefit the overall good of the organization. When we program our people to be thinking much more broadly than themselves, amazing things happen.

Finally, everyone should understand, internalize and actively practice respect. A lack of respect for the organization cannot be tolerated, under any circumstances. Disrespect is a one-way road out of town.

11

Do the Right Thing

—◈—

From early on in our lives, we are taught right from wrong. We are taught that taking a pack of gum without paying for it has ramifications and repercussions. The principles that guide our lives are intimately aligned with the principles that guide our businesses. We realize when we are doing something right and when we are doing something wrong.

Situations come our way in our workplaces that call for a choice to be made. There may be near-term benefits of making one call over another, but there will be long-term consequences for a poor decision. Aside from the obvious result of potentially losing your job, there is the less obvious but equally important result of irreparably harming your reputation among the people you report to and the people who report to you. Once you are marked "untrustworthy" or a person who crosses the line between right and wrong, it will be exceedingly difficult to shake that label.

Effective leadership calls for doing the right thing, every time. One bad move or ineffective (self-serving) decision will place you in a bad light with your team. One bad move can strip you of all the good you accomplished up until that moment. Your credibility must be without reproach at all times. Do the right thing, every time and without hesitation.

12

Be Careful Whom You Hitch Your Wagon To

—✍—

R aising children is no easy feat. We teach our kids right
from wrong and help influence who they choose as
friends. As a parent, it would be great if we could hand pick
all of their friends. We would certainly choose those who
have the right values, stay out of trouble, and are high performers in school. Choosing friends undoubtedly has a significant impact on the future direction and success orienta-
tion of your child.

As professionals, we need to be careful about the employees we choose to be associated with, for the same reasons.
We could be led down the wrong path, become negative, and
be viewed as flying counter to the direction of the organization. Our choices determine our path and ultimately could
have a significant impact on the trajectory of our careers.

When I was progressing in my career, two distinct leadership "camps" existed within my organization. I chose the

positive team. I chose the team that respected the organization rather than found fault with it. I chose the team that fostered teamwork and winning ways. In the end, good things happen to good people. Choose wisely and pick the team with the values that mirror your own. Hang with winners, and you will be viewed as a winner. Surround yourself with people who bring out the best in you, who make you a better version of yourself and who treat the company with complete respect.

13

Choose Your Generals Wisely

—⚏—

As a senior leader, you will be trusted to pick your team. This is a critically important responsibility and must be treated with great care. Your generals will be your right arm, your trusted confidants. Treated right, they will embrace and amplify your messaging. They will have your back, regardless of the pushback coming their way. They will align with your vision and facilitate complete alignment among their respective teams and the organization as a whole.

Having a loyal professional following is an absolute blessing. Knowing you have people who support you and the organization's mission is a key to success. Talent is hard to come by. Great talent is a real treasure. Align yourself with passionate, people-centric professionals who possess great character and values and who inspire greatness in others and never let them leave your side. Imagine interviewing for a new role, potentially outside of your current company, and mentioning that you don't come alone. How valuable might that be to your next employer? Building a strong leadership network is a key to being a great leader.

14

Checker-Upper vs. Helper-Outer

—⁂—

Early in my leadership career, I had a performance review in which I was told that, based on the way I run my business, I may be viewed as a "checker-upper" versus a "helper-outer." Talk about getting a kick in the gut! As painful as it was to hear, looking back on it, I realize that it was the best advice I could have received.

In a highly process-driven business environment, complete with daily individual meetings, pipeline reviews, daily activity reports, and cold-calling nights, you walk a fine line between being a "checker-upper" versus a "helper-outer." The key lies in defining the benefits behind each standard of the business. If we focus solely on "what" has to be done and miss out on the opportunity to describe the "why" behind it, we will fall into the dreaded "micromanagement" trap.

We all have processes within our respective businesses that, if left unexplained, will be viewed negatively. Every element is in place because it mitigates the risk in the business and leads to much better predictability, for both our reps and our organization. Take the time to explain the reasons behind the standards and what is "in it" for the employee (increased efficiency, better earnings, etc.). Once a person understands the benefit behind the action, alignment and acceptance are sure to follow.

15

Credit Giver vs. Credit Taker

—⟋ⱲⱲ⟍—

To be seen as true leaders, we must be conscious about the value of spreading praise where praise is due. How often do people shower praise your way, even though someone else had a big hand in driving that success? How many times could you have spoken up and deflected that recognition elsewhere instead of accepting that praise?

The "credit taker" is a person who may view the world as "dog-eat-dog" and practices an "every man for himself" philosophy. This person may focus on managing "up" and not realize the irreparable consequences on his team members for choosing the path of acceptance of praise while others are being overlooked.

The "credit giver" understands that sharing praise and showering it where it actually belongs is the right thing to do. People will view the credit giver as trustworthy, honest, and confident in who she is and what she stands for, both personally and professionally. The credit giver will be viewed as a leader.

This principle encompasses many of the topics previously discussed and many to come. Being a credit giver encompasses leading from the front, doing the right thing, placing focus on your people, and knowing whom you serve. The minute you veer from these principles, your credibility will be damaged.

Do the right thing every time and give credit where credit is due. Your team will respond to your confidence in the form of a tighter, deeper, and more trustworthy bond. Give 100 percent credit and take 100 percent blame. That is leadership at its finest.

16

First In, Last to Leave

—⚡—

Leading by example is a critical component to ensuring your position as a true leader. Our actions, rather than our words, will determine if we ever attain exemplary levels of leadership. We often see parents telling their kids not to smoke, only to light up minutes later.

In one of my earlier leadership roles, I was leading a team of nearly 100 sales, sales management, and sales support professionals. I had just taken over a division that had struggled for many years. In fact, it was ranked last among five divisions, and I was asked to turn the operation around. There were the obvious communication and vision/mission gaps, but I sensed a work-ethic gap as well. Having always practiced a strong work ethic, I was going to need to elevate it further in the hopes that the team would follow my lead. I had a parking spot right in front of the building where I always parked my car. I would pull in at 7:00 a.m. and park my car where everyone could see it as they came in for the day and went home at night. I never really talked about the need for people to come in early or leave late, I just let my car do the talking for me. One day, one of my managers parked in my spot before 7:00 a.m., and I was ecstatic! Now, this manager was a superstar with an incredibly strong work ethic. By his actions, he was telling me that it was time to raise the bar further. The next day, I came in at 6:30 a.m., and the game was on. Over time, our team members expanded their days, and we were off to the races.

Expanding days can work only if you lead by example. Raise that bar, and watch your team follow. Imagine if your team of eight worked an extra hour every day. That's an extra 40 hours per week, 160 extra hours per month, and nearly 2,000 extra hours per year. Imagine the success that would follow. I will leave this section by sharing one of my favorite quotes by Christopher McDougall, an American author and journalist who is best known for his 2009 best-selling book *Born to Run: A Hidden Tribe, Superathletes, and the Greatest Race the World Has Never Seen*: "Every morning in Africa, a gazelle wakes up. It knows it must outrun the fastest lion or it will be killed. Every morning in Africa, a lion wakes up. It knows it must run faster than the slowest gazelle or it will starve. It doesn't matter whether you're the lion or the gazelle—when the sun comes up, you'd better be running."

17

You Can't Be Half Pregnant

—◊◊—

Asked to define "commitment," management expert and author Ken Blanchard states, "There's a difference between interest and commitment. When you're interested in doing something, you do it only when it's convenient. When you're committed to something, you accept no excuses, only results."

Commitment lies at the core of the most successful businesses. It lies at the core of the most successful leaders and the most successful employees. Commitment is a state of mind, a firm and unwavering passion to see things through. Commitment is a promise, followed by action. It is a mindset. It is an attitude. It is a belief that it can and will be done, regardless of the challenges and adversity that present themselves.

As leaders, this commitment begins with us. It will resonate with our people if they see that we possess this commitment to excellence and to seeing the mission through. We must surround ourselves with people who carry this same trait. We are here to make a difference, and a difference can be made only when there is an unwavering commitment to making a difference. After all, you can't be half pregnant. You either are or you're not, and if you are, there is no turning back.

18

You Will Be Judged Based on Your Action or Inaction

—⟋⟍—

As a leader, you are constantly under a looking glass. Your boss is judging you, your peers are judging you, but most importantly, your people are forming an opinion, each and every day. With each decision you make, there are three possible outcomes: heightened credibility, harmed credibility, or neutral impact to credibility.

I recently read an article about a respected newscaster who was pulled over for drunk driving and had children in the car. This one action will likely cost him his job and could cost him his marriage. It will likely have a significant and long-lasting impact on the trajectory of his career and future income potential. Needless to say, this is an extreme example and certainly a significant lapse in judgment, which will have a major impact on this individual's life.

As leaders, this same thing can happen to us. How many times have we had a company outing at which we had a couple of drinks and decided to get behind the wheel of a car? If our people see this, they form an opinion of us. We must understand, like it or not, that we are always on display. Therefore, we must always conduct ourselves in a professional and responsible way. As leaders, we are never off the clock.

Here is another example. Imagine that we make a decision to hold on to an employee who is negative or disruptive—which is actually an inaction because we do not let the person go—or we make a decision to take some kind of action that is counter to the organization's mission or needs. We will be judged based on our inaction toward the disruptive employee and also on our action in making a poor decision.

Remember, every action or inaction has a resulting consequence tied to it. If we maintain a consistent approach, based on our internalized belief that the company trumps all, we will win the hearts and souls of our people, regardless of whether or not they agree with the decision personally. Consistency and alignment to the organization's mantra are paramount.

19

Act "As If"

—⁓—

I n the movie *Boiler Room*, Ben Affleck's character addresses a room full of future brokers. During his speech, he uses the phrase "Act as if." Now, I won't repeat the comments he stated because they were a bit off color, but the principle of the statement has stuck with me.

Wearing the "parent" hat for a minute, my wife and I use this strategy with our children. As they are heading out the door, we might say something like, "Act as if your grandma is with you," or to my eldest daughter, "Act as if your boss is watching." As you might imagine, these are impact statements and, at the right time, maybe later that night, it might cause both girls to pause and think before they act. It is certainly an impactful statement.

On the professional side, we can use this statement in a bit of a different way. When your employees approach you with a challenging situation, place them directly into the scenario, acting "as if" they were the boss. Acting "as if" they were the leader, while still in an individual contributor role, will allow them to view things differently, setting them up for what may be their reality down the road. Salespeople have a tendency to think differently than leaders, focusing their attention on individual needs rather than on broader company goals. Stressing the importance of acting "as if" they were in that next-level role will position them to reach that desired level.

If you are a front-line manager with aspirations to become a VP, start thinking like a VP. Act "as if" you are already in that role, and before you know it, you will be.

20

Act Like You've Been in the End Zone Before

—⚬—

I watch a lot of sports, and I am increasingly frustrated and embarrassed for those athletes who taunt, dance, and high-five their way around the field after making a simple tackle. Really? Aren't they paid to make that tackle, or catch that ball, or make that layup? I truly admired people like Larry Bird, Michael Jordan, Barry Sanders, Walter Payton, and Wayne Gretzky because they were respectful of the game they played and of those they competed against. You never saw these guys dance, or spike the ball, or go out of their way to place emphasis on themselves. They played the game the right way...with respect. They also asked for the ball. They wanted to take the big shot. They wanted to influence the outcome.

In my business, I watch salespeople tighten up at big moments. I watch them present smaller than they should and bring forward lesser programs than the client needs. At big moments, we need to take big shots. That moment, when we recommend our solution to our client, defines us as professionals. It is that moment when the client senses your confidence, much like a dog senses fear. It is that moment when your relationship falls apart or comes together. Confidence plays a key role in everything we do in life. Confidence is attractive. Confidence draws people in. Confidence breeds confidence. Confidence elevates careers. Confidence moves businesses forward.

Act like you've been in the end zone before. Look your client in the eye, smile, and ask for the business with complete and unwavering confidence.

21

Hire Passion, Teach the Business

—ɯ—

I n my business, I write a lot of job descriptions and review a lot of résumés. In my years at Monster.com, I spoke with hundreds of hiring managers and top corporate heads of HR. One stands out.

Enterprise Rent-A- Car was one of our largest clients. They had a specific and detailed process, much different than any other organization I had worked with. Enterprise was focused on one thing: passion. They were driven to find people who put themselves through school and accomplished things outside of school. And, while most companies focused on locating "A"-level students, Enterprise was focused on the "B/C"-level students. The grinders. Those with grit. They looked for passion, far and above anything else. They knew they could teach the business, but couldn't teach heart. Candidates either showed up with passion, or they showed them the door.

Passion is a common thread among the best and most talented people in every company. It is a requirement for achieving at an extreme level. Stop looking for experience. Find those with passion and teach them your business.

22

Will > Skill

—⚊—

In my career, I have been fortunate because I have qualified for President's Club twenty times. Qualifying for President's Club is quite difficult because this recognition is bestowed solely on the top 5 to 10 percent of a company's sales organization. Each time I attend a meeting, I do my best to spend time with each person, trying to understand what makes them tick. They come in all shapes and sizes while all possessing one key attribute: will.

Qualifying for multiple President's Clubs is a true accomplishment. Those who win multiple awards do so because they have "will" unlike others. They face the same adversity and challenges, yet they find a way to walk through them, go around them, or go over them. They get knocked down, but they get right back up. They keep coming.

Early in my sales career, I was keenly observant of those around me. I watched how people carried themselves. I watched how winners would win. I had a peer who was the most polished sales professional I had ever met. He was an incredible conversationalist, an amazing presenter, and incredibly smooth with his delivery. Words just seemed to come out of his mouth so beautifully. Even with all of these incredible qualities, this person never qualified for a President's Club award. As I studied him more, I found out why. Although he presented better than anyone else, he simply didn't do it enough. He would come in late, leave early, and outwardly share how busy he was. (Beware of people who always talk about how busy they are; likely, they are not busy at all). On the other hand, there was another rep who seemed to be on every award trip. He wasn't smooth, and he wasn't the best dresser. He simply worked…and worked…and worked. When others were heading out the door, he was hunkering down. He had grit. He was committed to winning. Given the choice, take will over skill every day.

23

"A" or "No Way"

—◊◊◊—

A lbert Einstein was quoted as saying, "Anyone who has
never made a mistake has never tried anything new."
Mistakes are an important part of learning, and organizations must test and challenge conventional organizational
wisdom. Organizations must make mistakes and learn (and
grow) from those mistakes because they often lead to other
great opportunities. Making mistakes is critically important
to the health, growth, and prosperity of the organization.
However, there is one area in which we should avoid mistakes at all costs: hiring.

Thirteen years ago, I made the conscious decision to hire
every person within my organization or, if we were in rapid
growth mode, at least have a conversation and review their
credentials. When we had a scheduled class on the horizon,
we would determine the markets where we would be hiring, and I would hit the road by myself or with my VPs. We
would divide and conquer. We established a process whereby
we would ask all candidates the same questions, use the
same personality testing, and administer the same interview

exercises. We also gave the candidates a bit of homework, asking them to send us an e-mail, that night, explaining why they were the right fit for the position and why they were the right person for the job. This final piece told us a lot—namely, could they meet a deadline, did they approach this exercise creatively, and were they passionate about the opportunity?

Effective leaders must be committed to walking away if something doesn't feel right. Hiring for an open position is not the goal. Hiring "A" players is the goal. We absolutely cannot miss in this area. Our company's culture and future success relies on our ability to be exemplary in this area.

Develop a process. Have your hand in every hire. Challenge your hiring manager if something feels off. Your team and your organization cannot make a mistake in hiring. Use "A" or "No Way" and be prepared to walk away. The near- and long-term health of your organization depends on it.

24

Hire People Who Don't Know
What They Can't Do

—⟶w⟶—

As discussed in the previous section, we often find ourselves looking for a certain person, from a certain company, with a certain level of experience. I would like to make a case that there is a better way and a more appropriate hire out there.

Hire people who don't know what they can't do. Sure, they lack experience, but they also lack bias, bad habits, and preconceived notions. It is certainly more risky to hire a less experienced person because he or she lacks a history of success, but you can elevate your expectations of that candidate because he or she has no point of comparison. It is like working with clay. You can mold the person to become the standard for others to follow.

Let's take a step back and talk about the "must haves" as you venture down this path. If a candidate has no history of professional success, we must look for success in other aspects of the candidate's past, whether through extracurricular activities during school or through philanthropy. We must dig deep in the interview process and pull out candidates' motivators, sources of inspiration, and role models. We must uncover the key intangibles of passion, grit, determination, response to rejection, drive, optimism, gratefulness, and generosity. Allow me to touch on the last two.

I hired a person for one of my sales roles who had never sold anything in her life. I have known her for more than seventeen years. Along the way, she has inspired me. She has an ability to connect with people that I have never seen before. She looks people in the eye, she genuinely cares, she truly listens, she places others needs above her own, she is grateful, and she is generous with her most important asset—time. All of these qualities lead to success in sales. She joined my team and instantly found success. Because she had no previous sales experience, she had no preconceived notions, no bias, and no bad habits. She didn't know what she couldn't do, and in turn, she found success and set a higher bar for her peers.

25

Great People, Mediocre Products; Mediocre People, Great Products

—ww—

The difference between a good and a great company sits squarely within the quality of its people. Given the choice to lead a team of great people with a mediocre product versus a team of mediocre people representing a great product, I'd take the former.

You see, with great people, you can accomplish great things, but with mediocre people, you will have mediocre results, regardless of the quality of the product or service you offer. Now, we'd certainly love to have both. But if that is not the case, we will most definitely focus on improving the area in which we are deficient. When you have a great team, it sets you up for greatness. It is easier to improve your value proposition when you have a strong team in place. Take the team and improve upon the proposition.

26

"No Jerks" Rule

—⁓—

I have an alternate title for this section, but I've chosen not to use it because I want to keep this book "G" rated.

Some of us spend more waking hours working than not working. We pour our hearts into our business and spend a great deal of time around our coworkers. To have a great company, we must have a great culture. To have a great culture, we must have great people. I am passionate about creating a culture that feels like a second home, that respects the organization and one another. One bad person can have a dramatic impact on the tone, character, and overall results of the company.

Ten years ago, I was brought in to run a large division of a company with a strong and recognizable brand. This particular division was not performing up to expectations and was lagging far behind the other divisions. After assessing all pieces of the business, I uncovered the problem: One person was getting in the way, and he happened to be the top salesperson on the team. He was disrespectful and egotistical, and he was padding expense reports and challenging the organizational vision. Overall, he was a real jerk. I approached my supervisor and let him know that I required his support because I was going to terminate this individual. He was surprised that I was going to displace the top rep on the team, but ultimately he became supportive when I presented the facts to him. I told him that I saw it as "addition by subtraction." I was confident that we would unlock the potential of the team by eliminating this overwhelming undercurrent of negativity—and we did.

Terminations are never easy and come with much emotion attached, but this one did not. When we hold the company in high regard, we must defend it with great vigor. As I mentioned previously, we will be judged based on our action or inaction. How could I garner the respect of my team members if I was reluctant to address such an obvious issue? Addition by subtraction. No jerks allowed.

Carve out the cancer before it infects the entire organization. Be quick and decisive. We work too hard to be surrounded by people who bring us down versus lifting us up. There is no room for people like that in a culture focused on respect, unity, and commonness of purpose.

27

Burgers and Beers

—⚮—

Over the past thirty years, I have had the opportunity to be surrounded by both great leaders and some who were not so great. Over time, you come to realize just how important it is to be tied at the hip with a strong leader. At this stage of my career, working with someone with great character, a shared focus on "team," and a passion and drive for success is a critical factor in my decision about where I choose to be employed. You have a choice, too.

Here's an easy way to determine if you are in the right place or making the correct choice in the next phase of your career progression. I use the term "burgers and beers." Now, not everybody eats burgers or drinks beer, so insert whatever you like in place of this phrase. The principle is the same. Could you see yourself going out for burgers and beers with this person who would be your supervisor? If the answer is yes, you have a fit. If not, dig deeper, and if you cannot find a point of connection, walk away. You need to focus on personal growth and happiness, and your supervisor has a direct hand in this. Although my personal success has never been hindered by the person I reported to, my happiness has been affected.

Earlier, I shared a story about a private equity firm assuming the leadership of one of my previous companies. After hours of speaking with them, I found no common ground and saw little hope that we could share burgers, beers, and laughs. Your connection with your supervisor can influence the rest of your life. If given the choice, choose your boss wisely.

28

Fail Fast

—⟋⟍—

We have a tendency to hold on to bad decisions about products, people, and processes well past their useful life. Face it, we all do it. "Fail fast" means that we should deal with the situation by ripping the bandage off quickly.

There are reasons we hold on to failing projects and people too long. First, if you had a hand in the decision, it can be humbling to admit to failure of an idea you had a direct hand in crafting. Second, if it is a people-related decision, it may be someone you referred or developed a personal connection with. Third, there is a whole slew of emotions tied to backpedaling from an idea or backing away from a person you supported.

However, there is an easy way to deal with it. The key is to think like an owner. If you are a leader in the business and you have internalized its mission, vision, and values, you are an owner. You have a fiduciary responsibility to make quality decisions that will have a positive impact on the trajectory of the company. You have to think in terms of the overall organization's health and the continued employment of all employees. Separate the emotion from the situation. Again, we should be making mistakes, or we're not trying hard enough. Failure feels like failure only if you let it feel that way, and nobody can make you feel a certain way without your approval. So fail fast and move on—the sooner the better.

29

High Standards Build Team Unity

—⟐—

L et's face it—high performers don't relate to mediocre players, and mediocre players don't relate to high performers. It's not that they don't like one another as much as it is that they don't have much in common with one another. High performers are committed to their personal and organizational goals. They are at the top for a reason. They are there because they want to be there, they expect themselves to be there, and they are willing to do what it takes to get (and stay) there.

Great organizations have standards, and high performers embrace high standards. Standards fall into two categories: standards that an individual expects of himself or herself personally and those that are built around communicated, understood, practiced, and consistent expectations that someone else has of an individual. Expectation standards may be based on activity metrics, conversion rate, or product sales. Holding your team to high standards focuses them on the important performance indicators that will lead them and the organization to success. Your high performers hold high standards today. Understand those standards and share them with the rest of the team. It's hard to argue against following the lead of the best people. After all, if it's being done, it can be done.

This is an area in which you should push the limits. If your team is performing at a certain level, elevate those expectations by focusing on the components that will drive results. You do not need to recreate the wheel here. Understand what the best do and hold the entire team accountable to those same standards. Imagine the overall impact on the organization when the new expectation is the bar set by the previous top rep. Remember, if it's being done, it can be done…by all.

30

Hitting Goal Is Failure

—⁓—

In order to be seen as the best and achieve at levels well above expectation, the leader must first fully embrace the concept that if we achieve what is expected of us, we have failed. When we were in school, a "C" was considered the minimum expectation. Achievers didn't settle for a "C", but rather focused on achieving at a much higher level. The same holds true in business, and it all begins with leadership re-setting the expectation.

This begins with a certain mindset and a definite mind-shift. It takes defining success and it must be communicated effectively and embraced thoroughly, by all levels. I personally believe that merely hitting goal is failure. A goal is the minimum expectation, much like the "C" in the classroom is. Achieving 120 percent+ is success. As soon as goals are communicated, we must immediately eliminate that thought and re-set to x+20%. Every rep and every manager must understand that the 120 percent+ level is considered the new bar and that anything below that it is considered failure. For the best of the best, the minimum expectation should be 150 percent to goal. This requires a mindset shift. I know this may seem like an extreme exercise, but it works, especially when we combine setting the expectation with consistent follow-up discussions with our people.

Earlier, we discussed the concept of WIIFM (what's in it for me). It is important, as leaders, for us to conduct both team and one-on-one discussions about what it means to achieve 120 percent of a goal or higher, in terms of compensation, personal growth, and advancement. That will help reps visualize the individual financial and career outcome that will result from achieving at that level. The key is to understand each person's individual needs and wants (new house, new car, etc.) and tie compensation to achievement of those personal needs and wants.

Print out a picture of each rep's goal and paste it near his or her desk for emphasis. It is imperative that we maintain focus on our goal at all times. All benchmarks and updates should be aligned with the 120 percent figure. All recognition should be tied squarely to the 120 percent figure, too. If a person falls short of 120 percent, keep him or her pointed at 120 percent and heading forward. This is purely a mindset, and everybody must buy into it.

31

Overpromise...Overdeliver

———✵———

We've all heard the concept of "underpromise and overdeliver." That is traditional and responsible logic, but the best leaders subscribe to the concept of over-promising and overdelivering. Although high risk can be associated with this principle, a case can be made that done right, careers soar as a result. There is something to be said about placing your reputation on the line, putting yourself out there, and then delivering on that commitment, while showing unwavering confidence along the way.

Now, I know this sounds irresponsible and potentially dangerous, but if we are to stand out and be viewed as best-in-class leaders, "underpromising" is a one-way ticket to obscurity. Overpromising and delivering on that promise is the type of legendary success that sets careers ablaze. If you have a team whom you trust and who trusts you, this serves as a true rally cry.

This concept also can have a dramatic effect on both team unity and overall organizational success in the long term. For it to work, you must have a high degree of confidence that it can be done, and you must have the manpower to pull it off. Again, your reputation is on the line, and forecasts are being communicated based on your commitment. You must be in control of your business and confident in your team's abilities. If you have a high degree of confidence, rally the team and take your shot. We're not placed on this earth to do merely what's expected of us but rather to accomplish the unexpected.

32

Win by a Dollar

—⟋⟍⟍—

S ales is a highly competitive field comprised of people who are driven to crush goals and step on anyone in their way, right? Although some people certainly may be like this, the vast majority of salespeople are respectful of their organization and their peers. As leaders, we have the responsibility to create a synergistic environment while fostering a competitive workforce. Most of the time, it is easier said than done.

For the organization to prosper, grow, and ultimately win, we must all win. One team, one goal. As leaders, we must be focused on ensuring the success of those we serve, in the form of every rep surpassing his or her individual goal. When each of us wins, we all win.

The goal is to strike a healthy balance between a competitive environment and a culture focused on supporting one another. To achieve this, we must drive home the point of winning "by a dollar." Although creating a competitive environment is important, it cannot be done at the expense of others. Again, we win only when we all win. Teach your team members to support one another while maintaining their competitive edge but to win only "by a dollar" over the next closest team member. Please understand that I am not implying that people should play "back to the pack." In fact, the goal is for everyone to win, at a very high level and have team members supporting one another in achieving that goal. The goal is for top players to pull other up with them and then continue their elevation and further pulling others up.

Focus your team on winning, and you will have achieved a critical component of success. Have your team members focus on winning by a dollar, and you will have fostered the healthiest of internally competitive environments.

33

Never Too High...Never Too Low

—⚏—

Life comes in waves; it is filled with many peaks and val-
leys. We must be able to grasp the fact that it all pretty
much levels out in the end. In sales, ebbs and flows come
daily. Being able to slow things down and maintain a consistent methodology and approach, regardless of the extremes
coming our way, is of true importance. We must keep our
emotions in check. We can never be too "high" or too "low."

Because I grew up in Chicago, I have been a lifelong
Chicago Blackhawks fan. In game six of the 2013 Stanley
Cup series, Chicago trailed Boston by a score of 2–1, with
just over a minute remaining in the game. The prospect of
returning to Chicago to face Boston in a Game 7 matchup
was becoming real. Within a matter of 17 seconds, Chicago
scored twice. When they were down 2–1, did they start thinking about Game 7? When they tied it up, were they resigned
to the fact that the game would go into overtime? This is a
perfect example of remaining in the moment, focusing on

your role, continuing to move forward and never wallowing in your current given situation.

We can find countless examples in sports of teams coming from behind against insurmountable odds. This happens because players are able to stay in the moment, slow things down, and continue forward with their game plan. Duke University basketball coach Mike Krzyzewski explains his amazingly successful "next play" credo: "In basketball and in life, I have always maintained the philosophy of 'next play.' Essentially, what it means is that what you have just done is not nearly as important as what you are doing right now. The 'next play' philosophy emphasizes the fact that the most important play of the game or life moment on which you should always focus is the next one. It is not about the turnover I committed last time down the court; it's not even about the three-pointer I hit to tie the game. It is about what's next."

Having the ability to maintain a consistent level of emotional output is what separates good from great—never too high and never too low.

34

Fly in the Radar

—∿∿—

G reat leaders place themselves in a position to be seen and noticed. Whether by their work ethic ("First In, Last to Leave"), their performance ("Hitting Goal Is Failure"), or through their ability to stretch ("Overpromise... Overdeliver"), they continue to be noticed because they place themselves in a position to stand out.

Flying under the radar is safe and may provide a level of stability, although that is arguable in these uncertain times. Great leaders put themselves out there. They volunteer for tasks that others shy away from, and they take on the challenges that cause others to hide. To stand out in a noisy and crowded field, you must fly *in* the radar. Be seen. Be heard. Get noticed.

35

Change Is Coming!

—⁂—

C hange is a way of life these days, and it comes at us in a multitude of ways. In the past year, it is likely that your company has experienced some changes, potentially in ownership, leadership, vision, direction, deployment, or compensation plans. These changes occur every month or potentially every week. If we are to survive and thrive, we must accept this fact and keep moving forward.

To cope with our ever-evolving environment effectively, first we must accept that it will be a constant in our lives. We also must understand that we need to remain focused on that which we can control. All of the items listed above are likely outside of the bounds of our control. What we can control is how we view the information we are given, what we do each day, and how we feel about the effort we put forth. If we go home each day feeling a sense of satisfaction that we have accomplished what we have set out to do, then we have no reason to feel any other way than satisfied. We did our job, and we did it to the best of our ability. We focused on our people, and we helped them further their careers. We respected our organization and moved our collective business forward. If we can stand tall and recognize that our efforts are powerfully aligned with the goals of our organization, then let the chips fall where they may. Finally, we can't control what other people think of us (and it's none of our business anyway).

Focus on your people, and the rest will take care of itself. Control what you can control, and do that well. After that, it's out of your hands. There is no use thinking about what may or may not be. Treat your business well, and chances are highly likely that your business will treat you well in return.

36

Be Relevant

—⟋⟍—

According to the Merriam–Webster dictionary, "relevant" is defined as "having significant and demonstrable bearing on the matter at hand." Your clients have choices. Every day, multiple salespeople approach business owners and decision-making managers with the intent of working with them. They are looking to grab a piece of the pie. Your pie. Staying relevant and visible among your top clients—those business owners and managers other salespeople are seeking out—will help you retain their business. You must uncover pain and opportunity and position your offering in a significant and relevant way. Tightly connect client pain to your offering and relevance will surely follow.

"Having significant and demonstrable bearing on the matter at hand" is a powerful phrase. Look at each of your clients and your average client value. Do you have a significant portion of your clients' overall "spend," and does it have a significant bearing on the success of your client's organization? Do your reps visit their clients regularly, with the intent of forming a real connection, or do they visit only when they want to sell something? Implement non-selling touches. Visit with the intent of anything other than selling. Relevance comes in the form of meeting the needs of the client, both within your offering, as well as the service you provide. Results, engagement and visibility drive relevance.

We see artists in the music industry come and go. One minute they are stars, and the next minute they are gone. They lost touch somewhere along the way. Someone better came along. They were no longer relevant. The same can happen to the relationships we have with our clients. Think "connect." Connections lead to trust, which leads to confidence, which leads to relevance, which leads to share of wallet.

37

Be Here Now

—⁓—

Our world has changed greatly over the past twenty years. I watched a video recently that talked about all of the things we used to do as kids that our children will never experience ("kick the can," playing outside all day, etc.). I know, my age is showing.

Today, our world evolves around technology. We have iPods, iPads, iMacs, iPhones, PlayStation, etc. The list goes on and on. Although I am a huge fan and supporter of technology, it can be quite distracting. In fact, it can be rather infuriating. I sit in meetings and watch people with their laptops open. Is it me, or is this disrespectful? Look around the next time you are in a restaurant or even walking around town. Notice the sheer number of people on their phones. I watch people at dinner, texting away, not even talking with their guests. They might as well be there alone.

Before every training session I conduct, I place the words "Be Here Now" on the board at the front of the room. I then define what that means. No phones, laptops closed, and complete immersion and engagement during our time together.

Focus on being in the moment in your personal and professional life, and help your team members see the value in doing so, too. When you are with your family, be fully immersed in them. Keep your phone in your pocket or in another room. Nothing is more important than that moment. Respect the situation and the people within it.

38

The Four P's

—◊◊◊—

Four key "must haves" define the cultural and competitive strength of an organization: people, passion, proposition, and process.

- **People**—From the moment a client, investor, or stranger walks in the door, your organization is being judged. What is the first impression at the reception station? How is the eye contact? What is the energy your team members are giving off? Are people smiling, and are they approachable? How would you rate the impression your organization creates?
- **Passion**—Is there passion within your organization? Can you feel it internally? Can strangers see it? If your spouse comes to visit, does he or she sense it?
- **Proposition**—Are you proud of the product or service your company provides? Does it bring real and tangible value to your customers? Is it cutting-edge? Can you articulate it? Are you passionate about sharing your story?

- **Process**—Is there structure within your business? Are well-communicated, well-documented, well-understood, and generally accepted standards in place?

We are all in a war for talent. Mastering these four areas will help you attract, grow, and keep talent.

39

Trust Is Front and Center

—⟋⟍—

Trust is at the core of any relationship. Personal relationships can flourish or end abruptly based on trust or a lack thereof. Countries can become allies or enemies based on trust or a lack thereof. Trust involves opening yourself up and exposing yourself to potential vulnerabilities. It is, in its purest form, an expression of care and connection.

As leaders, we must understand the significance of both placing our trust in others and having it granted in return. Trust cannot be required or requested. Trust must be earned. It takes months or years to earn, and it can be lost in seconds. Steven Covey defines trust as "equal parts character and competence." He goes on to say, "You can look at any leadership failure, and it's always a failure of one or the other."

Character is who you are and competence is what you do. Remember, you are always being evaluated. In any decision, assess the potential benefits and consequences. If you do the right thing consistently, focusing on your organization and your people, trust will remain front and center.

40

Build a Process

—꼬—

Our businesses contain key areas that need committed attention and a disciplined approach. Being diligent around each facet is imperative if we are to achieve success. Having a specific process outlined around each area is not only necessary, but critical to the success of your operation and to the organization as a whole.

Key areas requiring a disciplined process are recruitment, onboarding, new-hire and continued training, compensation, communication, reporting, recognition, and ranking.

When we are taught to set goals, we are told to write them down. Each element of each process must be written down and communicated to all. This is not an area where we can "wing it."

Identify your key areas, build out a process for addressing them, articulate it clearly to the organization, and follow it religiously. Success does not occur by accident. Success occurs by following a well-defined, well understood, and well practiced process.

41

Know Your Levers

—␣∿␣—

Every business has "levers," those areas where the equation for success can be found. In one business I was with, we used the equation DA x CR x DS:

1. **DA (daily appointments)**—About 60 percent of our business came from our local sales team in a high-volume and fast-paced business and nearly 35 percent of our local closes came during our first meeting. In this environment, a disciplined, activity-based lever was necessary. This was the most controllable lever, and we watched it closely every day

2. **CR (close rate)**—We would track appointments and conversions made during those appointments

3. **DS (deal size)**—We set an expectation around our average deal size and monitored it closely

There are likely two to three key levers in every business. If you know the areas that drive your success equation, you can monitor them closely, provide disciplined training around them, share best practices, maintain focus on them, compensate for them, and recognize performance within each area. Know your levers and how to impact each of them.

42

Know Your Metrics

———ﾆ———

F ollowing on the previous example, when you know your
  levers, you can manage and influence your business, and
your results will become highly predictable.

- DA (daily activities): 3/day/rep
- CR (close rate): 20%
- DS (deal size): $3,000

When you know your levers, you know your business.
When you know the metrics behind each lever, your business
will become predictable.

The numbers shown above made up our success equation. Every morning, we would run our Daily Activity Report
(DAR), which would outline the set activities for that day for
each rep. Once we knew the number of appointments, we
could accurately predict our results for that coming day.

Identify your levers and pull them. Know your metrics and influence them. Knowing your levers and metrics will drive your business.

43

Facts Are Our Friends

—⁓—

An old saying states, "You can't manage what you can't measure." I'll admit it: I'm a data junkie. The more I can understand about my business, the more I can influence it.

How often do we feel that we understand our business, only to receive data that shines a different light on it. Imagine going through your days and never truly understanding the data around your business. I would liken it to a baseball team not knowing its players' batting averages. A batter might think he is doing really well, based on his last few at-bats, or based on the week before, when he hit a home run.

The system known as "moneyball" was first implemented out of necessity when the 2002 Oakland Athletics and then General Manager Billy Beane were asked to field a competitive team while hamstrung by the franchise's challenging financial situation. By using a sophisticated approach to scouting and analyzing players called sabermetrics (the empirical analysis of baseball statistics), the Oakland Athletics set an American

League record by winning twenty consecutive games. The 2011 movie *Moneyball* chronicles this story.

Today, most teams have a metrics guru on its staff who assesses talent and develops in-game strategies. With facts, we have a line of sight into the specific areas of our business that drive success.

Dig deep into your numbers, and you will benefit greatly from the additional knowledge gained. Facts truly are our friends.

44

Rank Everything

—⁣♦⁣—

Television shows are ranked. Sports teams are ranked. Music downloads are ranked. Heck, even popular baby names are ranked. Salespeople and sales leaders want and need to be ranked as well.

Ranking success at your individual product level, as well as ranking your sales team, is an important part of understanding and influencing a business. Businesses traditionally have multiple product/service lines. Each of them should be ranked separately and the ranking sheets sent out on different days throughout the week, to give each product its own emphasis. Dress up the ranking, in order to give it a unique feel and send it out to the team accompanied by a note, recognizing the leaders of that line. As soon as you bring emphasis to individual product lines and couple that with recognition around that success, enhanced focus and results will follow.

Every business should have a robust and all-encompassing sales ranking as well. Individuals should be clustered by peer groups with criteria tailored to each individual group specifically. First, you must identify your key performance indicators (KPIs), which are the units of measurement that drive your business. In my last business, we had fourteen KPIs that included items like average bookings per month, average revenue per month, new business per month, average appointments per month, renewal rate, and retention rate. Each KPI was given a weighting (e.g., double weight, single weight, half weight) that emphasized category importance. Then each person was ranked within each category. Once all individual categories were weighted and ranked, we would add up all rankings by person and come up with an overall total by person and sort the list from lowest point total to highest point total.

We distributed rep rankings every Monday. We then scheduled one-on-one conversations between the managers and their individual reps, emphasizing strengths and areas requiring additional training and focus.

Ranking KPIs and people is essential to elevating business performance. If we place emphasis on key areas, they will become important, and focus and enhanced results are sure to follow.

45

Heat and Light

—⟋⟋⟍—

A plant requires heat and light to grow. A business requires the same to flourish. Bringing light to the darkness and attention to the important aspects of your business, will directly affect the trajectory of your results.

As leaders, we must understand every aspect of our business thoroughly. Again, as leaders, we have a responsibility to ensure the success of each of our people. To point them in the right direction, we must know where we stand and what success looks like. One way to do that is by ranking everything, as mentioned on the previous page.

Although facts are our friends, they can sometimes be painful to see. But we must bring focus to the results anyway; doing so allows us to influence those results going forward. We should not be judged based on the place where we stand now but rather where we head after gaining clarity. By concentrating attention on the individual pieces of the puzzle that will bring success, we can influence outcomes and elevate our business. This works only by committing to consistent communication and recognition of forward progress.

The key is to build a bridge between where we stand and the ultimate result we seek. By bringing heat (discussions) and light (transparency and visibility) to the forefront, we can bridge any gap and drive our results at the individual and collective levels.

46

People Buy from People They Like

—⚡—

Over the years, researchers have conducted numerous studies around why people buy certain products and why they buy from certain people and not others. There are key phrases and techniques that tend to work, but in general, people buy from people they like.

I reflect on the places where I shop. They are not the least expensive. They are not the most aesthetically appealing. They may not even have the best selection. I buy from those places because I feel comfortable there. I feel comfortable, because I have a relationship with and like the people I work with in those businesses. They know my name, they know what I like, and they seem to care about me as a person.

That is the key to business: Be a good person. Be a conversationalist. Be genuine. Be unique. Be authentic. Show genuine care. Smile. Set yourself apart.

47

Respect > Like

———〰———

We often see new managers assume their role and immediately work to be one of the crew. They want to be liked. Who doesn't want to be liked, right?

Although being liked is an important thing and helps us feel good about the relationships we have with our respective teams, it must follow respect in the equation. Focusing more intently on being liked than on being respected could lead to a team ignoring standards that are critical to the organization and skirting rules that help guide your business. It could result in a level of disrespect for your position, authority, and decision making. Respect sits at the center of the relationship equation. Respect comes from consistency in policy, continuity in decision making, predictability and reliability in following up on commitments, effective listening, and respective action. Leaders focus on the needs of their people.

By showing genuine care about your people and helping them through their challenges, you will gain their respect. Do the right thing for your people and your organization, lead from the front, and respect will surely follow.

48

Find Common Ground

—⁊⁊⁊—

We have all had people report to us who are very different than us. They have different interests, different goals, and a different way of viewing life. Effective leadership calls for finding common ground, which begins with finding commonality and being able to connect.

Being able to identify a connection point is what makes us great at sales and helps us in our personal relationships. We've all worked with difficult customers but have found a way to find a connection point and build from there. Sometimes it doesn't come easily; it can take a lot of work.

Earlier, I mentioned the principle of knowing whom you serve. Your reps are your clients. It is no different than when you sold, your customers were your clients; they dictated your success. Your reps are your clients and should be treated with respect, care, and your undivided attention. Sure, they're all different, but it is your responsibility to change, not theirs. You are the leader, and they are your clients. Finding common ground begins with an openness and a willingness to get to know people and to allow them to get to know you. Once you connect, the relationship can move forward and flourish.

Make your reps your priority and find a way to connect with each of them.

49

Balance Schmalance

—⁓—

By definition, balance means an "even distribution of weight." We often hear about balance in the workplace and how America is askew, compared to the rest of the civilized world. In America, we average thirteen vacation days per year, while countries like Italy, France, and Germany average more than thirty-five vacation days per year. The average American worker works 1,835 hours per year, which is more than Japan and most of western Europe. What's a person to do?

First, balance is a mindset. As Confucius stated, "Choose a job you love and you will never have to work a day in your life." Now, I know this saying is a bit overplayed, but I want to delve into it a bit. Let me start by asking a couple of questions. Do you make personal calls during the workday? Do you sometimes run errands during working hours? Do you cut out early from work sometimes? I'll answer the questions for you...yes, yes, and yes. I'll go one step further and state that you *should* do those things, and you should not feel guilty about it, as long as it's done respectfully and within reason. You see,

I don't view my personal and professional lives separately. Sure, there are different people in each group, and I have to be respectful of the needs of each group, based on meeting social and professional commitments. I simply toss it all into one big bucket called "life." I am blessed in my personal life, and I am blessed in my professional life and to me, they are all one in the same. Therefore, I don't get caught up in *when* I do things versus the fact *that* I do things. If I'm working from home and I want to take a walk with my wife in the middle of the day, so be it. On the flip side, when I'm working at 9:00 p.m. or on a weekend, I don't harbor ill will toward my company.

I believe that when you feel out of balance, it is because you are missing things that are important to you. When that happens, you become resentful. Resentment leads to a feeling of being out of balance. So, here's a solution. Make sure you don't miss things that are important. Ensure that you understand what is important to your people and ensure that they attend those events. When you're at peace and in harmony with your career and personal life, everything flows together, and there is no clear line of demarcation between the two. Although we certainly need to take vacations from work and consciously connect with our families, I fear that too much emphasis is being placed on "balance." Life is good. Think of both sides of the equation as equally satisfying. If your professional life isn't satisfying, then that's a different story. You owe it to yourself to find something that you are passionate about and pursue it. The balance comes with happiness and satisfaction, personally and professionally.

Finally, as I mentioned earlier, whichever side of the equation you sit on (personally or professionally) at any given moment, you owe it to your spouse, family, and organization to be "all in." Shut off the other side and focus on that moment and that moment alone. Be in the moment, and allow nothing to distract you from it.

50

The Team Will Flex as You Flex

—ⵑ—

Y ou are the leader, and your team looks to you for direction. Much like a child learns from his or her parent's
reaction by watching, your team will mirror your reaction to
circumstances.

Again, leadership entails owning decisions and embracing the organization's direction and vision. Effective leadership embodies "we" versus "they." Imagine, for a moment,
that you just came out of a big meeting in which changes
were proposed within the organization. You head back over
by your team, and they sense fear and anxiety. They see it on
your face. How might they react? Anticipate that they will be
anxious about the situation. While you are in the meeting, ask
questions. Gain clarity. Ensure that everyone in that room
shares a common talk track. This is the time to challenge
direction and get comfortable with the go-forward plan. The
minute you walk out the door, the company is king and you
own that direction, along with everyone else who was in that
meeting. You walk out with a smile, and your team will be at
ease. Inside, you may have some apprehension, but outside,

you focus on those whom you serve…your reps. When asked about rumors, keep your team focused on that which they can control. Keep them focused on those they serve… their clients. Do you see the common theme? If we focus on whom we serve and serve them well, everything else is secondary. Be conscious of your verbal and nonverbal communication. Smile and keep moving forward.

51

If It's Important to You, It Will Be Important to Them

—⚭—

With respect comes trust, and with trust you build loyalty. Whether discussing standards or elevated goals, if it is important to you, it will be important to your people because they care about you, and they trust in your direction.

As leaders, we inspire, collaborate, direct, and shape. Based on the connection we have with our team, we influence. Influence calls for the ability to alter direction without direct force. When we build trust, people will follow our path because they realize it is important to their leader and the organization, and as such, it will become important to them.

52

It's All Good!

—⁂—

In the mid nineties, M. C. Hammer released a song called "It's All Good." I conducted Monday-morning team meetings with 100 people at eight o'clock and would have this song playing as people came in the door.

I am a firm believer that we can convince ourselves to feel a certain way. Research shows that putting on a smile, whether forced or not, will allow the brain to send positive messages that will calm the mind and ease the body, thus lessening your stress level. Try it. It works. Nobody is in charge of your mood except for you. You alone control how you feel. Play music that stimulates. Take a moment and look around at the good in life. Take a deep breath and meditate. Preach goodness and find the positive in every situation. Although it is difficult at times, you can always find good. Tell yourself, "It's all good" because it truly is. Last I checked, the sun is shining, and if you're reading this book, you are six feet above ground, and that's something to feel really good about. Life is good and whatever professional situation you are facing, pales in comparison to your health and the health and well being of your loved ones. How often, when someone passes away, do you reflect and use the words "Boy, this really helps put things in perspective." It shouldn't take a catastrophic event to help you realize that you are blessed and life truly is good.

53

Your Grass Is Green

—⁓—

W e've all heard the phrase, "The grass is always green-er on the other side," denoting that opportunities elsewhere may be better than where you sit today. There are additional sayings that I believe are more accurate, like "Every lawn has brown spots; you just haven't found them yet."

When another company is courting you, there's no doubt that you feel good. Who doesn't like to feel wanted or impor-tant? Think back to when you first met a past girlfriend or boyfriend. The first few dates were really exciting, and then you noticed a mole you had never seen before, or you came across a hygiene issue that had never surfaced before. While seemingly shallow, we've all been there. Great early dates don't necessarily lead to the altar. Being able to sort through the emotional highs and dig deeper into the reality is para-mount in the decision making process. Often, candidates for a new job base their decisions on the visceral side alone, and that can spell disappointment and serve up the potential for additional job change in the future.

Every day, our people are being courted. It is our responsibility to help them see the light every day. To help them feel passion about their current role, first we must help them internalize the vision and embrace the future. Our goal is to make it difficult for our people to even accept that call, let alone go on that interview. We will undoubtedly lose good people, but it is our job to help them see that their goals are our goals and that we truly care about them, their career, and their future. Doing so will allow us to maintain talent. We must be focused on our people and their needs continuously. We must be outwardly focused. We need to be great landscapers and keep our lawns vibrantly green.

54

Ownership through Authorship

—◊—

How often do you make decisions without consulting with those affected and expect them to support it, embrace it, and run with it?

The term "ownership through authorship" allows the leader to set the tone, structure the initiative, and then include key people in the final details. Change is difficult, especially when it is thrust on someone. Allowing people to have direct input and help shape the final deliverable affords them a feeling of ownership. When a person owns something, he or she is more likely to support it.

Try forming a "council" made up of elected top reps within the business. Meet with them monthly and discuss issues facing the field. Use them to shape your standards and deliver them out to their peers. Not only will they feel challenged and appreciated, but their peers will more readily accept the edict when it is embraced by a respected peer versus the "boss." In addition, your council members will feel an intimate bond with the organization and pass when recruiters come calling.

55

Look Out the Windshield

—⚡—

Although learning from our mistakes is an important part of development and personal growth, we must keep ourselves staring ahead, looking out the windshield, instead of spending too much time looking out the rearview mirror.

Yesterday is gone, and tomorrow will come in due time. All we've been granted is today, and we must take advantage of that gift. It serves little purpose to live in the past because it is gone, and we can do nothing about what happened. What we can do is influence what lies ahead. There is limited space in our mind, and populating it with things that happened or things that might happen keeps us from focusing on what is happening.

56

Step Up vs. Pull Down

—⚡—

The top is a lonely place. It is much easier for people to pull you down versus elevating themselves to your level. Taking shots at you is easy. Stepping up is hard.

Top performers sit at the top because they work at it. They are committed to their goals, their organization, and winning. Unfortunately, not everyone is like them. Some people assume the worst of others. A rep might assume that the top performer had help getting to the top and that she was the anointed one...the chosen one. Had he looked over his shoulder as he was leaving the building at 5:00 p.m., he would have found the top performer settling in at her desk, immersed in her business, and taking care of her clients.

Those at the top must silence the noise and disregard those trying to minimize their achievements. As leaders of the business, we must be conscious that this takes place and monitor our environment closely. We must outwardly support those at the top by sharing their successes with the team. We must share best practices and allow others to see how things are being done. Providing a fully transparent view into success will allow others to see how they might be able to achieve at that level as well.

57

Reverse Robin Hood

—⁂—

R obin Hood was a historic outlaw known for stealing from the rich and giving to the poor. In Reverse Robin Hood, we flip the script.

Pay-for-performance compensation plans are essential for incenting the proper behavior, recognizing achievement that aligns directly with the company's mission, and moves the organization forward. The best way to influence performance is to prioritize it and address it through the compensation plan. If you want to make real change within your organization, you have to focus on it, especially in the area of compensation.

When developing a compensation plan, the coffers are not endless. We must make important and sometimes difficult decisions. Often, we spend time trying to craft the perfect compensation plan, only to neglect certain classes of people. Most of the time, these neglected classes are the people who possess the largest opportunity to stretch further, who get the most calls from recruiters, and who make the most significant impact on your team and your organization...your "A" players. Put simply, no matter what you are paying them, it is not enough. Someone out there will be willing to pay them more, and you cannot allow that to happen.

In this principle, we steal from the poor and give to the rich. We take dollars that we would appropriate to lower cut-in compensation points (e.g., payouts start at 70 percent to goal) and shift those dollars to the opposite end of the spectrum to reward over-delivery. In this example, we might structure the commission cut-in at 85 percent to goal and throw significant escalators to those who achieve at 120, 150, 200, and 250 percent (setting strategic stair steps that meet the needs of your business). With traditional plans, we have lower cut-ins because we fear that people might not get paid, should they have a rough quarter or month. If the quotas are too high, address that separately. If we feel that quotas are a stretch, but doable, we cannot cater to mediocrity. Instead, we must recognize and reward superiority. To truly elevate our organizations, we must feed the hungry and reward the rich. Your lower performers will step up, or step out, and you will keep your high performers squarely situated in the boat, right where you need them.

58

The Speed Of The Leader
Determines the Pace of the Pack

—m—

L eaders can have a great impact on their people and their organization, both positively and negatively. It all depends on the actions they take, day in and day out. It's about actions, not words.

Leaders are responsible for setting the tone, developing the mission, and inspiring their team members. Inspiration is short-lived in words. It is engrained in actions. People model their behaviors around those in superior positions within their organization. If a manager is coming in late, leaving early, and taking long lunches, so, too, will the team members. However, if a leader embodies the principles of coming in first and being the last to leave, spending significant time in the field with his people, sharing urgency, and using a "hands-on" approach to driving the mission, the team will follow. As leaders, we set the tone. The team will take on the personality we personify. We will cast the personal expectations we have of our people based on the high expectations we have of ourselves.

59

Focus on Activities, Not Results

—⚏—

R E/MAX holds an annual Long Drive Championship in Las Vegas. The world's longest drivers come together to display their amazing ability to drive a golf ball more than 500 yards. It's a pretty impressive event to watch. When those golfers set up for their drive, they are not thinking about the distance; they are thinking about the mechanics. They are thinking rotation, torque, balance, rhythm, grip pressure, release, and follow-through. If each component is completed correctly, the result will be a 500-yard drive or farther, a big trophy, and bragging rights for a whole year.

In business, we have a tendency to focus on the outcome rather than the components. For example, think about a sales call. Distinct elements must be followed to close a deal. A strong connection must be established early (and throughout the call). Detailed advanced planning needs to be completed. A lot of relevant questions and notes need to be taken. Pain and opportunity must be uncovered. We have to illustrate how our proposition solves the client's pain or capitalizes on the opportunity. We have to address concerns, then clarify, summarize, and hopefully close. Often, as I head into a meeting with one of my reps, I see a person focused on the outcome—the 500-yard drive—versus the components that will lead to the desired outcome.

In my last business, I mentioned that a significant portion of our business came from our local channel, which was a high-volume, fast-paced environment. We focused on activity, which was one of our three key levers and the component each person could control most easily. We didn't go into the day saying we needed to close $275,000 that day. We went into the day stating that we needed 450 appointments. We focused on the activity because we knew our metrics, and we knew if we had the appointment volume, the rest would fall in line.

Focus on the activity, not the results.

60

Strong Pace = No Stress

—✺—

I n the Kentucky Derby, the goal for a jockey is to clear the field, get out near the front, and control his pace. Rarely does a horse come from the back of the field and win the race. Pace is important in any race and in business.

Imagine being boxed out in the Kentucky Derby and having to dodge flying dirt, avoid shifting obstacles, maneuver your way through traffic and then make up significant ground. Not an optimal situation, to be certain. Much like a horserace, the goal in business is to set your team members up to win by being in control and out in front—from the start. A strong pace right out of the gate leads to reduced stress and an opportunity for a better outcome.

In a high-volume, fast-paced, monthly quota business model, every day is important. The best reps understand that "early and often" is at the cornerstone of their success. Waiting to pull out your goal in the last week is emotionally taxing and builds on a never-ending stress cycle. Imagine a rep who had a monster fourth week of the month. Come the first of the following month, he is still high-fiving him-self for his legendary close. At the end of the first week, he decides he had better get moving. By the second half of the second week, he is right back into stress mode and having to pull off a miracle again. God forbid if there is a freak snow-storm; he will be toast.

The best reps practice a principle known as "Groundhog Day." They treat every day identically by having three sched-uled appointments, regardless of whether it is day 1 or day 31. In strategic sales involving a longer sales cycle, activ-ity still plays an important role, but pipeline advancement equates to being in control. The goal is to have month 1, outshine month 3 in a quarterly quota system. Front-loaded success eliminates last-minute stress. It also helps reps avoid delays caused by people being out of the office or on vaca-tion and helps them avoid turning potential success into immense failure. Being in control plays a key role in dictating outcomes.

61

Goals Are Achieved One Bite at a Time

—␣␣—

During the first week of each year, I have an "all company" call. I share the company's vision, recognize successes, and position the great initiatives that lie ahead. Then I tell a story and roll out goals.

The last two weeks of December are a wonderful time of the year, a time of reflection. Reflection is an important exercise every salesperson should do regularly. Because we have monthly, quarterly, and annual goals, end-of-year reflection poses a unique set of challenges in sales. You see, sales is a grueling job, and it can take a toll on people. Staring at the prospect of starting all over again can be painful for many, which is why I tell the story of Sisyphus every January.

In Greek mythology, Sisyphus was a king condemned to a life of punishment due to his deceitfulness. Sisyphus was compelled to an eternity of rolling a huge boulder up a hill, only to have it roll back down once he reached the top. For sales professionals, February through December is the time they push the boulder up the hill. January 1st is the moment the boulder rolls back down the hill. As leaders, we must understand that this is the reality in the eyes of our people, and we must go out of our way to help each person through this internal struggle. I spent years at Monster.com leading our Enterprise sales team. Internal statistics showed enormous spikes in activity on our site during the final two weeks of December and the first two weeks of January, as people were actively pursuing other employment opportunities. We need to be on our game when the calendar flips to January, with a fully positive and inspirational assault.

Quotas are intimidating when viewed in their entirety but completely manageable when viewed as a result of our daily and monthly activities. The truth is, January 1 is no different than December 1 or July 1. If we practice a consistent daily approach, we will maintain control, and our results will flow consistently. We don't eat a sandwich in one bite; we eat it one bite at a time. The same goes for goals. Focus on the daily activity, and the goals will take care of themselves.

62

Bodies in Motion Tend to
Stay in Motion

—⚡—

A nd bodies at rest tend to stay at rest. As leaders, we must have standards and daily expectations to ensure that we generate momentum, maintain a rhythm, and keep our people moving.

Momentum is a really interesting phenomenon. When we have it on our side, we can seem to do no wrong. With every call and every meeting, things just seem to fall right. On the other hand, when things are off-kilter, or we allow that momentum to slip away, it seems that no matter what we do, things simply don't fall right. Calls aren't returned, and meetings end with a series of "no's" and "maybe's." Activity is at the core of maintaining momentum. We cannot allow ourselves, or our people, to spend too much time admiring our/their work. That high will drift eventually, and only active bodies can offset the low that inevitably will follow. It happens to all of us. The best baseball players go into slumps, and do you know what they do? They take extra batting practice and keep swinging.

63

The Fish Aren't Jumping in the Boat

—☾—

How often do we have salespeople who sit back and allow the brand to do the work and wait for leads to come pouring in? This can be a challenge to people who are new to sales who missed the point that they actually have to put themselves out there—cold call, knock on doors, and face rejection.

Sales is the one profession in which you face rejection a minimum of seven out of ten times. We need to hire people with a high degree of self-worth and confidence. People who are likable and optimistic. People who can handle rejection. We must instill a sense of purpose in our people and craft a road map to success for each of them. The truth is, waiting for the phone to ring will lead to certain failure. Salespeople must understand that activity is central to their success. They must practice alternate approaches (calling, dropping in, e-mailing, using social media, etc.). The fish aren't going to jump into the boat. Bites occur when we teach our people how to fish and hold them accountable to casting continuously.

64

You Can Outwork Any Challenge

—w—

You may not be the best presenter in your office. You may not be the most charismatic person in your company. You may not even dress the sharpest, speak the clearest or be the most handsome. Many of these are God-given attributes, and you either have them or you don't. One thing is certain, though: You can control your actions and activities. Derek Jeter said it best: "There may be people who have more talent than you, but there's no excuse for anyone to work harder than you."

Our role as leaders is to pick our people up, dust them off, and point them back in the right direction when they face adversity—and they will face adversity often. In recruiting talent, work to find people with resilience, people who have overcome major hurdles in their lives, people who demonstrate a strong work ethic. Resilience, the ability to overcome adversity, mental toughness, and an unwavering confidence and work ethic can be found in every winner, in every walk of life. We all face challenges. It is those who can maneuver through and around them who ultimately flourish. Although we may not be able to control everything, we can certainly control our view of a situation and what we are willing to do to overcome it. Top talent can outwork any challenge.

65

Storms before Rainbows

—◆◆◆—

F̲ew things are more beautiful than a rainbow; however, they don't come without a storm first. In business, sometimes we have to hunker down, ride it out, and muscle through, knowing that the end result will be worthwhile. How we choose to view adversity has a direct impact on our place in society and in business.

A Chinese proverb states, "It is better to light a candle than curse the darkness." We know that we will be faced with challenges and adversity. Rather than dwell on the challenge, face forward and know that good is around the corner. In previous sections, I have used the word "optimism." I believe this single characteristic lies at the core of every successful professional. Optimists have a knack for finding the good in every situation. Optimists realize that there is a solution, and they will locate it, hold onto it, and share it with others.

66

Manage to the Ledge

—⟶⟶—

We have people on our teams who possess a consistent sense of urgency. We also have people on our teams who do not convey a sense of urgency. It is our role, as leaders, to "manage to the ledge."

For a sales pro, a sense of urgency is as critical as a stethoscope is for a doctor or a hook for a fisherman. It simply needs to be there for things to happen. Managing to the ledge places responsibility with the sales leader to determine each rep's level of urgency and to push or pull the rep as a result. Manage each rep on to the ledge or off of the ledge. Allow me to explain.

In sales, there are three distinct types of reps: Those who are intently driven, intense, and never truly satisfied (I love these people, by the way); those who are driven to hit goal; and those who are satisfied with hitting a minimum commission cut-in and getting paid.

1. The intently driven, intense, and never truly satisfied reps, while likely great for the business, could
implode at any moment. They are driven to the
point that they walk a fine line between amazing and
self-destructive. These individuals need to be talked
"off" the ledge. Your conversation with these folks
is always assuring, complementary, and congratu-
latory but may end up very personal (e.g., calming
them, forcing them to take time off, listening to the
issues they are having at home due to their intense
focus). Practice sensitivity and compassion. No need
to worry about these people working; there is little
doubt that they are.

2. Those individuals focused on hitting goal make up
the lion's share of the people within an organization,
so there is great opportunity here. The focus needs
to be on moving the needle, not making drastic
change. They need a nudge to get up onto the ledge.
They have bandwidth, and they likely have skill. They
simply need to realize that achieving at quota, is not
acceptable, based on their talent level. They need to
understand that true success does not come in doing
what is asked of them (quota), but achieving at the
level of their capability.

3. Those satisfied with cutting into the minimum
threshold of getting paid, need to be placed directly
up on the ledge. They need a big old boost. They
need to understand that they are performing well
below expectations and well below their peer group
and that this is unacceptable and will not be tolerated. In no uncertain terms, they need to be given a

dose of urgency. "Good enough" to get paid is not good enough for the organization to thrive. "Good enough" does not pay the bills or cover all of the support teams and individuals who rely on sales to drive the revenue. Goal+ is the minimum expectation to remain gainfully employed in the organization. Drive them up on that ledge and make certain they stay up there. Be respectful but direct. Everyone needs to carry his or her weight and shoulder their fair share of the load.

67

You Have a Voice—Use It

—✹—

"Our lives begin to end the day we become silent about things that matter."

—Dr. Martin Luther King, Jr.

My wife and I are fans of the show "What Would You Do?" If you haven't seen the show, it places people in somewhat uncomfortable and potentially sensitive situations, and through a hidden camera, we watch to see if they get involved or they choose to do nothing. In our role as leaders, sometimes we find ourselves in difficult situations, facing a decision. This could come in the form of knowing that a person is doing something unethical or sitting at a table, being asked for your opinion on an important directional shift for the organization.

When we were appointed leaders, we were placed there because we had the right qualities. Our values mirrored the organizational values and our passion to help people aligned with the role of a leader. In assuming this role, we have a responsibility to our organization and to the people we represent, to do the right thing, to protect the interests of our organization, and to be a voice for our people. Regarding witnessing ethical misconduct, there is no gray area. Whether it is someone on your team, your best rep, or your boss, you have a responsibility to do the right thing. In the example of sitting at the table, being asked your opinion on an important directional shift for the organization, I will share a personal story.

Years back, the CEO of my organization was making a unilateral decision that I felt would have a significant and detrimental impact on the organization. I was not so sure that my opinion would carry weight, but I spoke up nonetheless. I spoke up because my people relied on me. They counted on me. I was their voice in that room, and I could not simply accept a direction that would impact the life of every employee within the organization. I spoke up knowing that, should we venture down this path, I could not be part of the go-forward team. I decided to move on from the organization that day. Now, that is an extreme situation, and it may not be right in your personal situation. The point is that we should all understand that being a leader is more than working with our people and helping them achieve their goals. When you sign on to lead, you have to be prepared to be "all in." Your organization and your people are counting on you. You have an opinion and a voice. Use it. You were chosen to be in your role for a reason.

68

Work on Your "Left Hand"

—⟋⟍—

For a fourteen-year period, spanning 1978 through 1992, my wife would tell you that I was the biggest Larry Bird fan around. In fact, the word "fanatic" would describe me perfectly. I admired his abilities, his willingness to take the big shots, his incredible tenacity, his obvious leadership, his complete selflessness, and his focus on the team.

Although he was a natural left-hander, Larry taught himself to shoot right-handed. Midway through his career, questions arose about his ability to drive to his left and shoot with his left hand. Teams thought they had found a flaw in his game. Larry worked on his left hand and became one of the best, if not the best, ambidextrous basketball player of all time. In fact, in a game on Valentine's Day, in 1986, against the Portland Trailblazers, Larry decided to finish every basket, other than a jump shot, with his left hand. He ended up scoring 47 points that night, 22 of them with his left hand.

The point of telling this story is that as good as we may be, we all have deficiencies. We need to identify our "left hand" (or "right-hand," for the lefties out there) and focus on being the best we can possibly be in that area. Life is about growth and improvement. Find your strengths and amplify them. Locate your areas of opportunity and develop them into strengths.

69

Be Authentic

—⚒—

When we talk about being authentic, we think about "walking the talk." We feel that if we follow through on our commitments, we will be seen as being authentic. In leading others, those around you judge your authenticity. You may feel that you are being authentic, but if others do not think you are, that is what matters.

Recently, my organization was going through significant changes, in terms of both ownership and strategy. I sensed tremendous uneasiness among the team, so I took to the streets to do roundtables with our various groups. I didn't have to do this, but I felt compelled. I knew how I would feel, standing in their shoes. The easy thing to do would be to sit back and let everything play out. The more difficult thing to do would be to face my people and have a frank discussion around where we stood as a team and as an organization. The team appreciated the transparency and authenticity.

People just want to know your point of view and get a feel for where you stand. Be honest. Be sincere. Be transparent.

After all, they are your team. You have a responsibility to be on the front lines and in the trenches with them.

When significant change occurs, it is fascinating to watch how people handle themselves. Some go into hiding, some start posturing, and the real leaders stay true to their commitment to focus on their people. That is our creed. That is our oath. We belong with our people, and we should experience change together.

70

No = Not Now

—⚡—

In sales, you face rejection all day, and you are expected to keep smiling, keep moving forward, and keep swinging doors. Seventy to eighty percent of the time, a salesperson is told "no," yet he or she keeps coming back for more. How do you keep from taking this rejection personally? How do you maintain confidence in yourself, both professionally and personally?

Research shows that 80 percent of sales are made on the fifth through twelfth contact, yet only 10 percent of salespeople make more than three contacts. Why is this? It's because rejection is painful, and we shy away from things that are painful. However, now that you know this stat, it will be easier to focus on influencing the way you operate going forward. Remember, facts are our friends.

Try this. Instead of thinking of "no," think of "not now." We have to internalize that people will eventually buy from us, even though we realize that not everybody needs our service or product. This is a mindset opportunity. Program your mind to see the "no," as "not now." Try to think that when prospects do not move forward with us, it is simply because we have not earned their trust yet. We need to teach our people to use "non-selling" moments to build trust among prospects. Have them drop by a prospect's office to drop off industry information. Have them drop by and say "hello" without making any reference to business. Touches lead to trust. Trust leads to business.

During annual meetings with our entire team, we would bring in clients and conduct a full question-and-answer session with them. I recall a restaurant owner who described his relationship with his salesperson. The owner mentioned that the rep came back seventeen times before he decided to do business with the rep. One of the people in the crowd asked, "Why so many times?" The operator stated that he has had salespeople walk through his door all day long and that they come in for only one reason…to sell him something. When he tells them that he is not interested, they walk out, and he never hears from them again.

Sales is a test of a salesperson's conviction, beliefs, and care for the business owner. If the rep truly believes that there is a fit between his offering and the client's needs, he will go back and visit the prospect until he finds common ground and until he and the prospect make the joint decision to partner.

If you believe, do what it takes to earn the trust and respect of the business owner, even if it takes seventeen tries.

71

Hero or Victim?

—ᴧᴧ—

We are the author of our own story and the writer/
director/actor of our own movie. We can choose to
be anything or anyone we want. We have cast ourselves as
the lead. What would we choose to be—a hero or a victim? I
would like to think that we would all choose the role of hero.

In our lives, we have the same choice. We can choose to
be the hero or the victim of our own lives. When we have bad
things that come our way, we have the choice as to how we
react to them. Much as the hero of the action film, we must
help our team members program their minds to understand
that there is a solution to every problem and a path to success. Help each of your people view themselves as a person
of purpose and as a person who makes a difference to those
around him or her. Help them view themselves as people
who can be counted on to help those around them. Help
them see themselves as people of substance, of character,
of principle. Being a victim is emotionally draining, both to
the individual and to those who surround the person. Being
a victim will hold a person back from reaching the levels they

seek and will certainly stymie their ability to advance in their career.

Build your team members up, and be prepared to pick them up when they fall. Remind them of their strengths and their purpose. Help them become heroes of their own lives.

72

Do, Versus Think

—⚒—

"The way to get started is to quit talking and begin doing."
—Walt Disney

For fifteen years, I have talked about writing a couple of books. I would jot down notes, make plans, write outlines, and then find a reason not to do it. "My life is busy," I would tell myself. "How can I find time to take on such a monumental task?" I would say. And then, something wonderful happened. I decided to prioritize what I wanted to do. I decided to take my career in a different direction. I decided to take action. Those are the key words: Take action.

For many years, I would watch leaders write solid business plans, only to watch them go in a drawer, never to see the light of day again. If we take the time to build a plan we truly believe in, what is standing in the way of us seeing it through? Is it self-doubt? Is it the amount of time and energy necessary to make it come together? Is it complacency? Are we overthinking? Taking action is an act of will. It requires that we commit to moving forward, regardless of the energy required or the challenges presented.

As Ken Blanchard states, "There's a difference between interest and commitment. When you're interested in doing something, you do it only when it's convenient. When you're committed to something, you accept no excuses; only results." If you want something badly enough, you will find the time to make it a priority.

So stop making excuses, build that plan, implement it, and see it through.

73

The Script Is Your Ally

—⚏—

In September 1985, I committed to joining R. H. Donnelley as an inside sales rep. Two weeks before my start date, I was handed a script and told that I needed to memorize it by my first day. On my first day of new-hire training, I was required to write a thirty-two-page script. If I could not perform this task, my offer for employment was going to be withdrawn. Welcome to the world of scripts.

This example is certainly extreme, but it shows a commitment to a proven process. In sales, the best organizations leave little to chance. From what you say, to how you say it, to when you say it, to how often you say it, a solid plan leads to predictable results.

I'm a big movie buff and have lots of favorite actors. Sean Penn, Mel Gibson, Denzel Washington, Brad Pitt, and Daniel Day-Lewis are among my favorite dramatic actors. As natural as their delivery comes across, every word is scripted. The writer and producer do not allow variation. The actors are required to recite the script, word for word. It doesn't seem that way because they work to bring a natural element to it.

If you are in a business that requires a script, embrace it, emphasize it, and achieve perfection around it. It was likely built by a team of people who have uncovered the path to success. Follow the leader here. Your business and results will benefit from your commitment.

74

Inspect What You Expect

—⚏—

P rocess in place, check! Script, check! Activity standards set, check! Plan developed and communicated, check! We're ready to go, and then…we are pulled sideways, and our new hire is thrust into the field, on his or her own.

In putting a detailed process in place, we must ensure adherence. To do that, we must uphold our end of the bargain, as leaders. If we are committed to the process, we must let nothing keep us from executing on it. Assuming you have daily calls/meetings scheduled with every person on your team, you should block that slot out and commit to those discussions. Nothing is more important than the success of your people. We have a responsibility to train our people, communicate our expectations, and keep them tight to the centerline…that place where everything is in line with what has been trained, communicated and expected. Over time, veering slightly off of centerline will undoubtedly result in failure. Stick to the standards. Stick to the process. Commit to the success of your people. If you *expect* adherence to the plan and the process, *inspect* adherence to the plan and the process.

75

Visualize

—⚹—

Elite athletes have used visualization for many years to form a mental imagery of the event about to take place. They see themselves entering the starting block, feel the wind and the calm before the starting gun goes off, initiate that initial burst, then mentally run the race and cross the finish line. By going through this process stage by stage, the athlete relaxes and physically steps into that exact sequence. With mental rehearsal, our bodies and minds can actually perform at the desired level.

Early in my career, I learned to visualize the call I was about to attend. I would close my eyes and envision walking into the business, shaking hands, and sitting down. I would visualize the inside of the office and the client I was about to meet. I would mentally go through the call. I would see the client's reactions, hear the objections, and come to a point of resolution. Many times, the call would play out as I had envisioned it. Visualization is a powerful tool. It provides clarity and sharpness to the situation and calms the body and mind, thus allowing for peak performance.

76

Challenge the Position, Not the Person

—⚹—

Disputes are going to take place in your workplace. You may be in the middle of one right now. Ineffective communication takes place when we attack the person versus the position that person represents.

Challenging a person may occur as a result of a buildup of emotions over time. Effective leadership calls for separating emotions and feelings and addressing the person's stance or position on a given topic, rather than attacking him or her directly. Eliminate your perception and bias and focus on the position. Challenging a person rarely leads to progress. Focus on what moves your business forward. We have limited time in the day, and harboring negative feelings keep us from representing our people and our business in the best possible way.

Tackle the issue, keep moving forward and keep personalities out of it.

77

Focus on the Bookends

—◊—

To affect your business, you must focus on maximizing your team's available work week. No, I'm not asking for people to work later or to work weekends; I'm simply asking them to work their weekdays. The three most productive days of the week are Tuesday, Wednesday, and Thursday. There is a reason for this. We allow our employees to use Mondays and Fridays to do "office work." It's time to get back the bookends of the week.

By allowing your employees to use Mondays and Fridays as office days, or days to catch up on paperwork, you have effectively reduced your team's productivity level by 40 percent. Time is our second most important asset, behind people, and we have allowed 40 percent of it to walk out the door. I believe that if you give people additional time, they will find a way to fill that time, and not always productively. Do a time–motion study on what your average rep does each day. Really try to dig deep and understand. By going through this process, you will uncover a multitude of ways to help your team members with their efficiency and overall effectiveness.

I've personally been on more than 10,000 enterprise, agency and SMB-level sales calls and have found that 90 percent of calls last less than one hour. If we work eight hours in a day (likely more), isn't it reasonable to expect three of those hours to be spent in front of a client? That would leave a minimum of five hours to prep, set future appointments, make cold calls, do paperwork, travel, etc. Sounds reasonable, right? So why do we need office days? Holding your team members accountable for five days of client activity will afford each individual fifteen meetings per week. If we allow office days, we would only capitalize on nine calls in a given week (three calls/day for three days/week). If we have a closing metric of 20 percent, fifteen meetings per week would equate to three closes per week, while nine meetings would equate to 1.8 closes per week. Over a year, fifty weeks of field activity would add up to sixty additional closes for the person who works five days, over the person who was in the field only three days per week. Last I checked, we are in the business of driving revenue, and that is an everyday requirement. Maximizing productivity and time in front of customers, is a must.

78

Differentiate

—⁓—

"Regardless of age, regardless of position, regardless of the business we happen to be in, all of us need to understand the importance of branding. We are CEOs of our own companies: Me Inc. To be in business today, our most important job is to be head marketer for the brand called You."

—Tom Peters

Tom Peters is an expert in business management practices, and he hits the nail on the head here. Whether with your clients or internally within your company, you must develop, hone, and work on the brand known as "You." By creating a brand, you will create demand. Imagine if you were starting a new company in a competitive field. Undoubtedly, you would set yourself apart. You would stand out in that crowded field. You would issue a press release, create a vibe, and work to be recognized as the best in your field.

I would propose that there is no difference between launching a company and enhancing your personal brand. People buy you (or not) every day. What are you doing to improve your personal brand? How are you helping your people develop their personal brands with their clients? It starts with focus. It starts with differentiation. The easiest way to start is to immerse yourself in the person you are speaking with. Be distraction-free when involved with your reps and clients. Be genuinely interested in people, be passionate about their needs, and always think about giving versus getting. Unfortunately, many focus internally and are short on their outward focus.

By consciously taking a keen and committed focus on others, you will be taking the first (and biggest) step toward differentiation.

79

Pips Help People Get Better, Not Get Fired

—⚹—

Performance Improvement Plans (PIPs) are in place to bring a structured and disciplined approach to improvement of a poor-performing employee. There is a popular misperception that a PIP is the first step in displacing an employee who doesn't belong in your organization. If we head into this process with that way of thinking, the person will be set up for failure, and that would be a disservice to our employee, ourselves, and our organization.

Think back to the last person you placed on a PIP. Now, I want you to think back further, to the time when you first hired that person. You had a great interview. You saw passion and excitement. You saw the fit. Your organization invested significant dollars bringing this person on board, through initial training, continued training, benefits, your time allocation, etc. Now you are at a point where there is a disconnect. The results aren't there, and you are turning your focus away and toward those who are giving effort and want to be there. This is a common every week/month occurrence.

The truth is, some people are simply bad hires. We have to fail fast and move forward. However, for the majority of PIPs, it is a situation in which a person was once a contributor and has since veered off the rails. I'd like you to think about something: Did you do all you could to help that person along the way? Were you there for her when she needed you? Did you have her best interests in mind? Did you invest in her with your time, compassion, passion, and true care? Every time I place somebody on a PIP, or one of my leaders places one of his or her people on a PIP, I sit back and I think about these things. I reflect. I take it personally. I owed them my best. Did I give it to them? Placing a person on a PIP is a chance to correct any bad habits and re-engage myself in that person's life. It is my chance to step in, step up, and help. During the PIP period, I commit myself to the person I am working with. Throughout that period, we both own their success, and I will know I gave it everything I had. The PIP allows us an opportunity to get a person back on track and show them that we genuinely care about his or her success.

80

Explain It to Me Like I'm A
Four-Year-Old

—⚉—

If you can't explain it simply, you don't understand it well
enough."

—Albert Einstein

In the movie *Philadelphia*, Denzel Washington is an attorney representing a dying client (played by Tom Hanks).
Denzel Washington says, "Explain it to me like I'm a four-year-old." I love this line. How often do you ask someone
what they do for a living and after they explain, you still have
no idea what they do? How often do you explain your offering to a client and you see a glossed-over look on his face?
Business does not have to be complex.

Pretend you are explaining your business to your four-year-old. Dumb it down. Keep it simple. Simple sells.

81

Storytelling and Hammocks

—⁓—

What child doesn't love story time? She cuddles up in her bed, pulls the covers up, and Mom or Dad pulls out a book and tells a story. To a child, this is a good as it gets. In my career, I have sat through thousands of presentations, but I would grade only a few as engaging, exciting, and enthralling.

As sales professionals, we are taught to engage, connect, uncover, and share. The problem is, we tend to spend more time on the sharing part and not enough on the three previous and most critical components. More than I care to admit, I hear things like, "Tell me about your business," followed by "Great! Now let me share how my company can help." Now, this may be an extreme example, but scary enough, it's not too far removed from the truth. Among the very first things I do when I join a company is immerse myself in the people and the proposition. I want to understand how we are unique and how we share our uniqueness internally and with clients. I get in the field and I observe. I then break apart the proposition and put it back together in an easy and engaging way.

At Monster.com, our meetings entailed presenting in front of executive teams via PowerPoint. We made the conscious choice to eliminate slides that talked about us and replace them with slides that talked about our clients. We created slides that were visually appealing, with very few words. We focused on presenting our clients' needs and illustrating how our offering could align and assist with their points of pain and opportunity. We added exercises and levity into the deck to keep the room out of the dreaded "hammock," where the presentation starts strong and then lulls the attendees to sleep shortly thereafter, only to spike at the end again.

Find your uniqueness through your presentations. Focus on the "why," versus the "what." Tell stories, infuse an element of fun, and make them memorable. Be unique. Be authentic. You have one shot to impress. Make the most of it.

82

Proofread 3x

—◠◡◠—

I have a pet peeve. I'm not sure where it comes from; it possibly emerged when I was a child. I'm sure having a wife and daughter as educators may have driven me to this point as well. I am amazed at the number of grammatical and spelling errors I receive on a daily basis, through e-mail, from people above me, people who work with me, people who want to work with me, and people trying to do business with me. It is truly astounding.

We all make mistakes. As particular as I am about this, I, too, make mistakes (and it kills me when I'm called out for it!). There is an easy solution here. First, turn on spell check. Second, proofread three times. Slow down. Look for grammatical errors. Remember, your reputation is gold, and you will be judged (deliberately or subconsciously) based on your care and attention to detail. I have chosen not to hire people and not to do business with people because of sloppy grammar. If a person is going to be this careless with something as important as their career, or earning my business, then I can only imagine how they might handle a big project or an important meeting, once we become co-workers or partners.

Your credibility is on the line. Be a pro. Proofread three times.

83

Take On the Biggest Bully

—⚡—

In the holiday classic *A Christmas Story*, the mild-mannered Ralphie decides he is tired of being picked on and decides to fight back, taking on the neighborhood bully, Scut Farkus. This is a classic scene and a great reminder of how rewarding it is to take on what appears, on the surface, to be an unwinnable challenge and actually pull it out.

Back in 2012, I was presented with a couple of great opportunities with great companies to head revenue for their respective organizations. One company was in growth mode. Things were going well. They were prepared to scale and needed to double down. There was no doubt that this was going to be a winner. The other company was part of a large publicly traded organization in the midst of a proxy fight in which the largest single investor was looking to gain board seats and shutter the business. I watched closely as the CEO stood ground with great confidence and passion and fought back the attack. I did my research and uncovered countless articles about the impending demise of the business. There were about one hundred negative articles and predictions of failure for every positive write-up.

When I met the team, I saw drive and ambition. I saw a company that believed in the future. I saw a proposition that was powerful and needed in the community, and I felt a deep passion for the path ahead. I knew the risks going in. I had my eyes wide open. I chose this path. It was the challenge I wanted. It was the test I needed. There was an easier path, but I believe we are not put on this earth to take the easy path but rather to take the path that will help us grow and test ourselves. I didn't want to be on my deathbed, at the close of my time on this earth, and know that I took the safe route, the easy path.

Choose the path that tests you, that challenges you. Take on the biggest bully.

84

Zig When They Expect You to Zag

—⚶—

Y ou can learn a lot about leadership by watching press conferences following big games. We've all seen coaches point fingers at both referees and players. We've seen classic meltdowns. We've seen blank stares. I am most impressed when I see a coach congratulate the other team and stand behind his players. This is leadership at its absolute finest and the basis of "Zig when they expect you to Zag." What you do in times of adversity will define you as a leader.

Imagine that you just closed Q4 and your team missed goal badly. The effort was there, but the results were not, and the questions start coming from above. Do you make excuses and point blame at particular players on your team? Or do you accept the blame, share your go-forward plan, and deal with whatever consequences may follow? How do you approach your team in that situation? They are certainly expecting emotion and potentially a beat-down. My recommendation, as difficult as it may be and as counterintuitive as it may feel, is to take the opposite approach. Embrace in times of pain and press in times of good.

When people lose, they need support, especially when they put forth a strong effort. Winners are harder on themselves than you can ever be. They need your embrace. They need to feel your support. When teams are winning, press. In sports, most teams lose their momentum, and potentially lose the game, when they rest on their lead and play back on their heels.

The time to press is when things are good. Drive the team. Maintain and build on the momentum. Zig when they expect you to zag.

85

Put Yourself Out There

—⚍—

"Don't become something just because someone else wants
you to, or because it's easy; you won't be happy. You have to
do what you really, really, really, really want to do, even if it
scares the **** out of you."

—Kristen Wiig

We all have a comfort zone, and we live safely and
securely within that zone, pretty much our entire
lives. We think about things we want to do, whether start a
new business, change the course of our career, or move to a
distant land. We start with great passion around it and then,
over time, it loses steam and we settle back into our comfortable routine. In sales, we refer to this as "Time kills all deals."
If a client doesn't act swiftly, the business likely will not be
won.

The start of a new year is a good time to "recreate" one-
self. Do something different personally and change something about the way you do things at work. Let it be notice-

able. It may be a new process, a new tactic, or a completely new approach. Just do something.

Also, self-deprecation, done right, can relieve tension, draw people in tighter, bring your personality to light, and simply open yourself up to people. At our big company meetings, we would have karaoke one night. I have dressed as Lady Gaga and Katy Perry. For those who know me, that is really putting myself out there. Don't be afraid to put yourself out there. Letting your guard down is a good thing, and your team will have some fun along the way.

86

Give to Get

—⚡—

People buy from you because they like, respect, and trust you. However, it didn't start that way. There was likely avoidance, distance, and apprehension. You had to work at finding common ground, establishing a connection, and building trust.

At Christmas, I love to give, far more than I love to get. My wife is exactly the same way. We enjoy bringing happiness to others. Upon reflection, I believe this has helped in my career. Although closing sales is a part of a salesperson's life, it never felt like selling to me. Instead, it felt like giving. Much like a doctor would identify symptoms and areas of pain and then prescribe a remedy, I would feel the same way about my profession. I would identify areas of pain and opportunity in a business and then prescribe a remedy. I never felt like I was peddling. I always felt like I was giving.

Sales is a challenging profession. Business owners and corporate decision makers are approached daily by people touting their wares and trying to "sell" them something. To be successful, you must differentiate yourself. You must be unique. You must stand out in a crowded field. Try this: Focus on giving something versus asking for something. Bring a client something of value. I don't mean a gift; I mean a news article, a publication, something that would bring value to their role or their organization. Refer them talent for an open position you came across. Do something without expecting anything in return. Often, you *get* when you're focused on *giving*. Focus outward.

87

The Land of Maybe

—⁂—

S ales is a black and white thing—either someone buys
or they don't. At all costs, we must avoid the "Land of
Maybe."

The goal of a salesperson is to build trust and develop
a relationship. Throughout the process, there is an ebb and
flow. Maneuvering and directing this flow is a key component
in determining whether a relationship will develop or not.
When reviewing pipelines, how often do your find the same
opportunities, in the same place, week after week? If this is
happening, you are officially in the land of maybe. Either
opportunities advance through stages or they are stuck. With
effort, we may be able to move them, but if they sit there
too long, they become stale. They are not real, and it is time
to make a call.

Rather than shudder at the idea of peeling opportunities
off of a pipeline, some reps would rather hold on to false
hope. As leaders, we need to teach the principle that "no" is
actually a good thing. It allows reps to know exactly where

they stand, not where they hope they stand. It allows them to focus on real opportunities and not waste time on long shots that have little hope of coming to fruition. Most importantly, it allows them time to affect their outcome while they still have time. "No" is a good thing, and "maybe" is a bad thing.

Avoid the land of maybe at all costs.

88

Take It Like a Man/Woman

—∭—

Personal accountability is the act of being able to answer for the outcomes of your actions, your behaviors, your decisions, and your results. Being able to answer to others is part of it, but being able to answer to yourself is an even more important key to understanding and practicing personal accountability.

The beautiful thing about sales is that it is 100 percent objective. You have a goal, and you either hit it or you miss it. You will be judged accordingly. You will be applauded for success and questioned on failure. Strong professionals understand and accept this. It is par for the course. The challenge comes in dealing with those who avoid taking responsibility and accountability for their actions and results.

Be true to yourself and self-reflect on what you could do better and what specific steps you can take to improve. Embracing accountability strengthens relationships, builds trust, and makes you stronger.

If you are terminated as a result of missing a sales goal, accept it and move forward with your head held high. Turn the page, accept responsibility, learn from the challenge, and point no fingers. It's about you and nobody else. Accept that as a fact. Point inward.

89

Listen!

—∭—

"Most people do not listen with the intent to understand; they listen with the intent to reply."

—Steven Covey

In new-hire training, I make it a point to spend extended time with our new employees. During my session, I ask, "What is the most important trait of a salesperson?" I usually hear things like the ability to close, activity, drive, and ambition. Those are all worthy attributes, but they pale in comparison to mastering the ability to truly *listen*.

I love the above quote by Steven Covey because it is so true. Most people listen with the intent of capitalizing on a gap in the conversation so that they can ask their next question, or they are half listening because they are focused on what they are going to say next. In fact, more than ever, interrupting is becoming the norm. I'd go as far as to say that it is becoming an epidemic. People are hurried and worried that they might forget what they are going to ask. They're fearful that their time will be cut short and forget to ask pertinent questions. They are nervous that there may actually be a gap, an awkward moment, in which nobody is speaking. They jump in, disrespect the speaker, and interrupt the conversation.

Listening is the absolute key to connecting, forming a bond, finding pain, and uncovering opportunity. Imagine if you went to your doctor and told her you have a pain in your side. Would she ask you to lie down, pull out her scalpel, and start cutting you open? No. She would ask a series of questions, and she would listen intently to your responses. She would take notes and ask further questions, depending on your answers. She would slow things down. She wouldn't be in a race to prescribe a procedure. As sales professionals, we are negligent, and we open ourselves up to "malpractice," if we assume we have an answer before truly understanding the pain and the situation.

Slow down the selling process. Ask relevant questions. Listen and formulate follow-up questions based on the answers you hear. Clarify and listen more. Listening is an art. Consciously practice this art.

90

Think Before You Speak

—⚹—

"I've learned that people will forget what you said, people will forget what you did, but people will never forget how you made them feel."

—Maya Angelou

Take a look at any successful team, and you will find a team that practices effective communications. Positive, challenging, and sometimes emotional exchanges will occur, but they will be done with respect and a conscious understanding of the other person's feelings. Where there is genuine care, there is respect and control.

I will share a secret with you. Pause, gather your thoughts, and think about how the other person may *hear* you, rather than how you want to say something. This tactic requires that you focus on the other person. It takes a conscious effort. Often, communications break down because our focus is on how we are feeling, when they should be on how the other person will interpret what they are about to hear.

Slow down, gather your thoughts, and think about the other person. You'll be glad you did, down the road.

91

Great Questions Lead to Great Connections

—⁓—

When you find a great sales training company, use them and take them with you wherever you go. I have one such company. Tom Cooke, president of Learning Outsource Group, uses the phrase, "Tellin' ain't sellin'; asking questions is." Nothing could be truer.

If you couple great questions with active listening, you will have the one–two punch that legends are made of. It is the front half of the meeting that determines the outcome. When done right, the "close" is simply a natural extension of a strong line of questions, great listening, and the forming of a connection. The close is not an "event," it is the beginning of a relationship.

Asking great questions and actively listening and reacting to the answers, will drive connection, bring light to the need to work together and establish long-term and fruitful relationships.

92

Nobody Cares What You Did

—⚬—

You were a star salesperson last year and got the tap on the shoulder to become a manager. It was an exciting day. You couldn't wait to get started and meet your new team. In your first meeting with the team, you began by talking about your successes. You started telling the team about how you used to do things. You told them how great you were, "back in the day." You sounded like Uncle Rico from the movie *Napoleon Dynamite*.

When you become a leader, the word "I" needs to be eliminated from your vocabulary—immediately. You have to understand that it is not about you any longer. It is now squarely about the team. It is not about how great you were; it is about how great you will make your people. You work for them. They do not work for you. Shift your thinking from "me" to "we." Nobody cares what you did. They care only about what you can do for them now.

93

Don't Tell Me About the Labor
Pains; Just Show Me the Baby

—◆—

I can't tell you how many times I have been approached by team members who tell me about how much work they put into a particular project, or the sleepless nights, or the obstacles they had to plow through. And how many times I watch reps go to their clients and tell them about the "strings they had to pull" to get them the result they were looking for.

In business, we are here to get things done. We are here to accomplish goals. Our job is to bring a favorable result forward. Sure, there are going to be bumps and challenges. Sure, we are going to have to rely on others who didn't uphold their end of the bargain. In the end, we have a job to do, and if we're committed to the people we serve, no obstacle is too great and no wall is too high to scale.

So the next time you want to tell someone about how much you had to go through to deliver on a request, just smile and think about labor pains and babies. Do your job and deliver on your commitment, regardless of the hurdles that lie ahead of you.

94

Discipline Is Not Something You Do to Someone; It Is Something You Do for Someone

—∿—

Between 1991 and 1998, the Chicago Bulls won six NBA Titles. Between 2000 and 2010, the Los Angeles Lakers won five NBA titles. Two completely different teams, with completely different players, led by one man—Phil Jackson.

Phil Jackson had a belief that his process, when implemented, would deliver championships. It would take hard work. It would take the right players. It would take discipline. Phil Jackson needed the right players. He needed stars, but he also needed role players. He needed people who were focused on the good of the team versus individual glory. He needed people who would consider themselves one of fifteen versus one of one. Phil's process would take discipline, but the result would be worth the effort. Phil Jackson led two separate teams to eleven NBA titles over a nineteen-year period.

Often people view discipline as a negative, when it is the discipline that brings structure to chaos and success to individuals and organizations. Success comes from winning. Winning comes from following a well understood, repeatable and predictable process.

95

What to Do When You Want It More

—⁄⁄⁄—

Our teams are made up of a blend of people at various levels of ability and performance. We have some "A" players (hopefully), some "B" players, and likely a few "C" players and below. It would be great if we had a team made up solely of "A" talent, but unfortunately, that is seldom the case. We also have people who outwardly exhibit passion and enthusiasm for our products, our clients, and our business. With others, we may have to work harder and dig deeper to find and pull forward that passion. What do we do if we don't find that drive, that fire, or that passion? What do we do if we want success for a person more than he wants it for himself?

If a person is not performing well and is exhibiting signs of complacency or the fact that he's satisfied with subpar performance, it's time for a discussion. Share your feelings and try to uncover that rep's needs, wants, and motivators. Try to find a way to tie success to attaining the things he wants. It might be a car, a new place to live, or the ability to provide further for his family. If he is satisfied with his sub-par performance, we must help him understand that we have minimum standards and they come in the form of quota attainment+.

We spend more than half of our waking hours working. Happiness, challenge, growth, and internal gratification must be in play, or it's time to move on. Our people must commit to making an impact. Give me a person with will, and I can help him. Give me a person with skill and lacking will, and he cannot be helped.

The moment you notice that you want success for one of your people more than he wants success for himself, something's got to give. Someone's got to go, and it shouldn't be you.

96

Hard Work vs. Smart Work

—⟋𝕨⟍—

E arly in my career, I took great pride in my work ethic. With my chest out, I would think, *Nobody can outwork me.* One day, a supervisor said to me, "Don't confuse hard work with success." That statement has stuck with me ever since.

Eighteen years ago, I was running a one hundred-person team in the suburbs of Chicago. We had turned around a struggling division and built a great team. We were producing significant and consistent results. We had a weekly ranking sheet that ranked peer groups, including divisions. We were the top-ranked team, but another division was on our heels every week. They would take the top spot for a week, and then we would regain the top spot. This would go on for months. I would hear that my counterpart would work out in the middle of the day and didn't possess the same work ethic I possessed. I couldn't imagine that this competitive division could achieve that level of results without putting the hours in. I knew what I was putting into my business, and I couldn't fathom that anything less would garner a comparable level of results. I then thought back to the supervisor who spoke with me about confusing work ethic with results. You see, my counterpart had it figured out. She could achieve great results with less effort because she had a strategy, whereas I had muscle. She had a plan, whereas I relied on energy. She had it right. I had it wrong.

Work ethic, while important, is only part of the equation. You must have a plan, a process, a detailed approach, and a synergy and alignment among the troops. Working smart, coupled with working hard, is the equation for sure-fire success.

97

Slide Aside

—◆—

"Give a man a fish and you feed him for a day. Teach a man to fish and you feed him for a lifetime."

—Chinese Proverb

B ack in the day, when we were selling, we were the bomb! Nobody could outsell us. Give us the most challenging opportunity, and we would close it. We were regular legends in our own minds. Today we are tasked with building teams. We are responsible for developing our people and helping them grow and flourish. Then why, when we are in the field with our people, do we jump in and take over a meeting? *Slide aside*, we think. *Let the master take over.* Do we need this for our ego? Do we believe this action will build trust and confidence in us as leaders? True, we are in business to drive revenue and make money. Also true is the reality that our reps will benefit from increased commissions based on our involvement on a call. However, we are not in business solely for the near term. We must be focused on all terms (near, mid and long).

We are in the field for a day with a rep. We must be focused on the days when we are not in the field with that individual. Our time in the field is to be spent listening to the rep, connecting, partner selling, demonstrating, role-playing, and providing feedback. Our responsibility is to catch our reps doing something right and to build on that find by reinforcing the positive parts of the way they run their business. We are there to encourage, assist, and further develop them so that they become self-sustainable when they are in the field alone.

98

The Buffet Line

—⁂—

An African proverb states, "It takes a village to raise a child." In other words, it takes more than one person to teach a child the ways of life. The child comes across many people and, in doing so, learns right and wrong from listening to and observing others. This section follows the same principle.

As I write this book, I think back on the many great leaders I have had the opportunity to work with. From them, I learned how to (and not to) act. I viewed every situation as an opportunity to learn. Leadership mirrors the buffet line. The buffet may have ten salads, ten entrees, and ten desserts. Some may appeal to you, but others may not. So you head down the line, tray in tow, and you pick the things that appeal to you while leaving the unappealing items behind. This mirrors our professional lives. As you continue to progress in your career, be open to what is being presented to you daily. People are brought into your life for a reason. You can and should learn something from every person and every interaction. Sometimes you learn what *to* do and sometimes you learn what *not* to do and both situations will bring immeasurable value. Life brings great lessons forward. Embrace tactics that that will make you a stronger leader. Make those uncovered processes and attributes part of whom you become going forward.

I want to close this section as I began, with a quote. Mother Teresa said, "Some people come into your life as blessings. Some people come in your life as lessons." Be thankful that you have crossed paths with those who have been placed in front of you. Every person brings value your way. Some you recognize immediately, and some you realize over time. Learn. Adapt. Adjust. Grow.

99

Be Humble...Be Confident

——

"For everyone who exalts himself will be humbled, and he who humbles himself will be exalted."

—Luke 14:11

There aren't many more powerful quotes than that, huh? That pretty much says it all. Confidence is necessary, but humility is paramount.

Carry yourself with great conviction, with a focus on helping others and deflecting versus accepting credit. When you focus outward, amazing things will come your way. Relish the success of others, while downplaying your own success.

100

Always Be Grateful

—ɯ—

"It is not happy people who are thankful. It is thankful people who are happy."

—Unknown

Several times per week, I send inspirational notes to my team. Some are funny and some are serious. The majority of them focus on being grateful. It is easy to be distracted in our lives and to focus on the noise and events that are thrust upon us each day. We have to understand that those things will be there, but we must consciously be in the moment and realize how amazingly blessed we are. When you are filled with gratitude, good things come in abundance.

As for me, I'd like to share what I am grateful for, in the hopes that it will inspire you to conduct the same exercise.

I am grateful for the life I have been given. I am thankful that I have been given the gift of this day. I am thankful that the sun is shining. I am thankful that I have found my soul mate and the love of my life. I am blessed with an amazing family and health among all of us. I am humbled with the love that I have surrounding me each day. I am thankful that my family has a roof over our head and heat to warm our home. I am thankful that I live in America and that we have peace in our country. I am thankful that I am six feet above ground. I am truly blessed.

Find the good in every situation. It's there. Sometimes you just have to slow down, be in the moment, eliminate the noise, and take a look around. You'll be amazed at what you actually see when you consciously slow down and deliberately look around.

101

Choose Happiness

—✶—

Happiness is a choice. Every day, we can choose to stay in bed or spring out of it. We have a choice about how we view the world and the people who live within it.

Remember that happiness comes when we focus outward. When we give to others. When we commit to generosity with our time and whatever resources we can provide to others. Live a grateful life.

I leave you with my Six Rules for Happiness:

1. Love
2. Eliminate hate and worry
3. Family is all that truly matters
4. Look for the good in people
5. Go out of your way to help others
6. Slow down, decompress, and *smile*

About the Author

Jim Lipuma has been leading sales teams for nearly thirty years. He has worked for Fortune 500 companies, as well as pure start-ups, turnarounds and companies focused on exponential growth. Jim has led teams as large as 300, with multiple levels of sales, sales management, sales marketing and sales operations and revenues exceeding $250 million annually. Most recently, Jim was SVP, Revenue for Patch Media (an AOL company). Jim also has held the positions of Chief Sales Officer for Restaurant.com and VP of Sales for Monster.com, Imagitas, and R. H. Donnelley.

Made in the USA
Charleston, SC
27 April 2014